America's Infrastructure and the Green Economy

Other Books of Related Interest

Opposing Viewpoints Series

Automation of Labor
Development, Land Use, and Environmental Impact
Labor Unions and Workers' Rights

At Issue Series

America's Infrastructure
Environmental Racism and Classism
The Federal Budget and Government Spending

Current Controversies Series

Domestic vs. Offshore Manufacturing
Fossil Fuel Industries and the Green Economy
Sustainable Consumption

> "Congress shall make no law … abridging the freedom of speech, or of the press."
>
> *First Amendment to the US Constitution*

The basic foundation of our democracy is the First Amendment guarantee of freedom of expression. The Opposing Viewpoints series is dedicated to the concept of this basic freedom and the idea that it is more important to practice it than to enshrine it.

America's Infrastructure and the Green Economy

Eamon Doyle, Book Editor

Published in 2023 by Greenhaven Publishing, LLC
29 E. 21st Street
New York, NY 10010

Copyright © 2023 by Greenhaven Publishing, LLC

First Edition

All rights reserved. No part of this book may be reproduced in any form
without permission in writing from the publisher, except by a reviewer.

Articles in Greenhaven Publishing anthologies are often edited for length to meet page requirements. In addition, original titles of these works are changed to clearly present the main thesis and to explicitly indicate the author's opinion. Every effort is made to ensure that Greenhaven Publishing accurately reflects the original intent of the authors. Every effort has been made to trace the owners of the copyrighted material.

Cover image: Chandra Ramsurrun/Shutterstock.com.

Library of Congress Cataloging-in-Publication Data

Names: Doyle, Eamon, editor.
Title: America's infrastructure and the green economy / Eamon Doyle, book editor.
Description: First Edition. | New York, NY : Greenhaven Publishing, 2023. | Series: Opposing viewpoints | Includes bibliographical references and index. | Audience: Ages 15+ | Audience: Grades 10-12 | Summary: "Anthology of essays examining and debating the status of America's infrastructure and the possibility that a green economy as a solution"-- Provided by publisher.
Identifiers: LCCN 2021055640 | ISBN 9781534508798 (library binding) | ISBN 9781534508781 (paperback)
Subjects: LCSH: Infrastructure (Economics)--United States--Juvenile literature. | Environmental economics--United States--Juvenile literature. | Environmental policy--Economic aspects--United States--Juvenile literature.
Classification: LCC HC110.C3 A5395 2023 | DDC 363/.0973--dc23/eng/20220124
LC record available at https://lccn.loc.gov/2021055640

Manufactured in the United States of America

Website: http://greenhavenpublishing.com

Contents

The Importance of Opposing Viewpoints	11
Introduction	14

Chapter 1: Are the Potential Benefits of the Green Economy Worth the Risks?

Chapter Preface	18
1. The Green-Collar Economy Is Booming *Christina DiPasquale and Kate Gordon*	20
2. The Bipartisan Infrastructure Bill Won't Create Jobs as Advertised *Brad Polumbo*	25
3. There Is a Demand for Analytical Skills in a Green Job Market *Rakesh Kochhar*	28
4. Green New Deal Legislation Is Bad for the Economy and the Environment *Nicolas Loris*	33
5. How Many Green Jobs Are There in the US? *Karlygash Kuralbayeva*	37
Periodical and Internet Sources Bibliography	41

Chapter 2: Can the US Afford to Improve Its Infrastructure with a Green Economy?

Chapter Preface	43
1. The Overall Cost of Green Reform Matters Less Than How We Pay for It *Edward Barbier*	45
2. Carbon Pricing Should Play a Major Role in Green Reform *Grant Jacobsen and Carolyn Fischer*	50
3. The Green New Deal Is a Left-Wing Boondoggle *John Kristof*	62

4. The Green New Deal May Boost Carbon Emissions 67
   Matthew Paterson
5. There Are Various Problems with the Green New Deal 72
   Steven F. Hayward

Periodical and Internet Sources Bibliography 77

Chapter 3: Can a Green Economy Drive the Economic Growth That America Needs?

Chapter Preface 79

1. Degrowth Policies Cannot Avert Climate Crisis 81
   C. J. Polychroniou
2. Green Economic Growth Is Real and Thriving 90
   Lucien Georgeson and Mark Maslin
3. Green Growth Is a More Tenuous Proposition Than Advocates Suggest 94
   Manu V. Mathai, Jose A. Puppim de Oliveira, and Gareth Dale
4. A Green New Deal Makes Economic Sense 105
   Sophie Carter

Periodical and Internet Sources Bibliography 109

Chapter 4: Is a Green Economy Beneficial to American Businesses and Investors?

Chapter Preface 111

1. Investors Should Embrace the Scope and Scale of the Green New Deal 113
   Daniel Stewart
2. Investors Can Take Advantage of the Green New Deal 118
   Michael Kahn
3. Green Reform Poses a Unique Set of Challenges for Small Business 124
   Addisu Lashitew

4. Businesses Should Prioritize Sustainability Investments **138**
   Shalini Unnikrishnan, Chris Biggs, and Nidhi Singh
5. Relying on Green Consumers Can Be Risky
   and Challenging **144**
   *Katherine White, David J. Hardisty, and
   Rishad Habib*
6. The Business Community Can Help Manage the Transition
   to a Cleaner, More Efficient Economy **159**
   Sanya Carley and David Konisky

Periodical and Internet Sources Bibliography 165
For Further Discussion 166
Organizations to Contact 168
Bibliography of Books 172
Index 174

The Importance of Opposing Viewpoints

Perhaps every generation experiences a period in time in which the populace seems especially polarized, starkly divided on the important issues of the day and gravitating toward the far ends of the political spectrum and away from a consensus-facilitating middle ground. The world that today's students are growing up in and that they will soon enter into as active and engaged citizens is deeply fragmented in just this way. Issues relating to terrorism, immigration, women's rights, minority rights, race relations, health care, taxation, wealth and poverty, the environment, policing, military intervention, the proper role of government—in some ways, perennial issues that are freshly and uniquely urgent and vital with each new generation—are currently roiling the world.

If we are to foster a knowledgeable, responsible, active, and engaged citizenry among today's youth, we must provide them with the intellectual, interpretive, and critical-thinking tools and experience necessary to make sense of the world around them and of the all-important debates and arguments that inform it. After all, the outcome of these debates will in large measure determine the future course, prospects, and outcomes of the world and its peoples, particularly its youth. If they are to become successful members of society and productive and informed citizens, students need to learn how to evaluate the strengths and weaknesses of someone else's arguments, how to sift fact from opinion and fallacy, and how to test the relative merits and validity of their own opinions against the known facts and the best possible available information. The landmark series Opposing Viewpoints has been providing students with just such critical-thinking skills and exposure to the debates surrounding society's most urgent contemporary issues for many years, and it continues to serve this essential role with undiminished commitment, care, and rigor.

The key to the series's success in achieving its goal of sharpening students' critical-thinking and analytic skills resides in its title—

Opposing Viewpoints. In every intriguing, compelling, and engaging volume of this series, readers are presented with the widest possible spectrum of distinct viewpoints, expert opinions, and informed argumentation and commentary, supplied by some of today's leading academics, thinkers, analysts, politicians, policy makers, economists, activists, change agents, and advocates. Every opinion and argument anthologized here is presented objectively and accorded respect. There is no editorializing in any introductory text or in the arrangement and order of the pieces. No piece is included as a "straw man," an easy ideological target for cheap point-scoring. As wide and inclusive a range of viewpoints as possible is offered, with no privileging of one particular political ideology or cultural perspective over another. It is left to each individual reader to evaluate the relative merits of each argument— as he or she sees it, and with the use of ever-growing critical-thinking skills—and grapple with his or her own assumptions, beliefs, and perspectives to determine how convincing or successful any given argument is and how the reader's own stance on the issue may be modified or altered in response to it.

This process is facilitated and supported by volume, chapter, and selection introductions that provide readers with the essential context they need to begin engaging with the spotlighted issues, with the debates surrounding them, and with their own perhaps shifting or nascent opinions on them. In addition, guided reading and discussion questions encourage readers to determine the authors' point of view and purpose, interrogate and analyze the various arguments and their rhetoric and structure, evaluate the arguments' strengths and weaknesses, test their claims against available facts and evidence, judge the validity of the reasoning, and bring into clearer, sharper focus the reader's own beliefs and conclusions and how they may differ from or align with those in the collection or those of their classmates.

Research has shown that reading comprehension skills improve dramatically when students are provided with compelling, intriguing, and relevant "discussable" texts. The subject matter of these collections could not be more compelling, intriguing, or urgently relevant to today's students and the world they are poised to inherit. The anthologized articles and the reading and discussion questions that are included with them also provide the basis for stimulating, lively, and passionate classroom debates. Students who are compelled to anticipate objections to their own argument and identify the flaws in those of an opponent read more carefully, think more critically, and steep themselves in relevant context, facts, and information more thoroughly. In short, using discussable text of the kind provided by every single volume in the Opposing Viewpoints series encourages close reading, facilitates reading comprehension, fosters research, strengthens critical thinking, and greatly enlivens and energizes classroom discussion and participation. The entire learning process is deepened, extended, and strengthened.

For all of these reasons, Opposing Viewpoints continues to be exactly the right resource at exactly the right time—when we most need to provide readers with the critical-thinking tools and skills that will not only serve them well in school but also in their careers and their daily lives as decision-making family members, community members, and citizens. This series encourages respectful engagement with and analysis of opposing viewpoints and fosters a resulting increase in the strength and rigor of one's own opinions and stances. As such, it helps make readers "future ready," and that readiness will pay rich dividends for the readers themselves, for the citizenry, for our society, and for the world at large.

Introduction

> *"It is possible to chart a course towards a green economy that sustains decent new jobs. But it requires realism, seriousness and attention to detail."*

Since the late twentieth century, environmental and ecological science have played an increasingly important role in public policy debates on topics ranging from industrial regulation and municipal zoning to infrastructure development and the exploitation of natural resources. Green values like conservation, sustainability, energy efficiency, and responsible consumption have achieved influence in the business community and across the field of economics. Prominent US politicians have embraced reform platforms like the Green New Deal (GND), which seeks to implement green values in the development of a more environmentally sound economic system. President Biden's Build Back Better initiative, which focuses on upgrading and improving America's physical infrastructure, exemplifies the green movement's growing influence.

But the green movement has also created controversy, some of which derives from major challenges that are inherent to green reform. The political scientist Matthew Paterson explains:

> The Green New Deal contains a basic contradiction that anyone pursuing it will have to wrestle with as it develops. Many of the measures proposed—such as investing in infrastructure and spreading wealth more evenly—will intrinsically work in tension with efforts to decarbonise the economy.[1]

Green reform plans also tend to generate opposition from a variety of powerful interest groups, many of which have a stake in traditional industries like oil, manufacturing, and transportation. Interests based in these industries often perceive the green movement as a threat to future opportunities and growth potential because of the movement's focus on reducing carbon emissions and industrial waste.

Critics also cite the public cost associated with major reform plans like the Green New Deal and Build Back Better. But perhaps the most politically salient line of concern derives from the possibility that green reform could lead to major upheaval in the job market. Sarah O'Connor of the *Financial Times* explains:

> The truth is that the road to "net zero" will destroy jobs in some carbon-intensive sectors, even as it creates new ones elsewhere. And some activities will not need as many workers as before. […] It is possible to chart a course towards a green economy that sustains decent new jobs. But it requires realism, seriousness and attention to detail.[2]

Most advocates of green reform will readily admit the scale of the challenges associated with transitioning to a cleaner, more efficient economy—but also insist that major action is well worth the cost.

Opposing Viewpoints: America's Infrastructure and the Green Economy explores four areas in the broad and highly complex debate about climate change, infrastructure development, and economic reform. The first chapter surveys the impact of green reform on the job market and the various risks and opportunities that new, proactive climate policies present for American workers. The second chapter covers different perspectives on the cost of aggressive green reform initiatives like the Green New Deal and the question of how to pay for them (with taxes, through deficit spending, by reducing spending on other programs, etc.). The third chapter asks whether green reform and innovation have the capacity to drive economic growth at the level required to sustain the overall prosperity of the US economy. The fourth and final chapter looks at the impact of climate policy and green reform on the landscape of opportunity for private business and investment. The range of perspectives represented in these chapters is intended to illustrate the enormous complexity involved with implementing a comprehensive green reform plan like the GND and to enumerate both the risks and opportunities that would accompany a cleaner, more sustainable economy.

Notes

1. "The Green New Deal's Contradiction—New Infrastructure and Redistribution May Boost Carbon Emissions," by Matthew Paterson, The Conversation, March 6, 2019, https://theconversation.com/the-green-new-deals-contradiction-new-infrastructure-and-redistribution-may-boost-carbon-emissions-112078. Licensed under CC BY-ND-4.0 International.
2. "Not All Blue-Collar Workers Will Find Green-Collar Jobs," by Sarah O'Connor, *Financial Times*, May 4, 2021. Reprinted by permission.

CHAPTER 1

Are the Potential Benefits of the Green Economy Worth the Risks?

Chapter Preface

One of the main areas of controversy when it comes to climate policy and green reform involves potential disruptions in the job market that could result from aggressive climate action at the national level. A green revolution could theoretically produce millions of new jobs, but huge numbers of American workers are employed by firms in the fossil fuel industry and in various sectors across manufacturing, retail, and transportation. The perception among many who make their living in these industries is that policies aimed at reducing carbon emissions or incentivizing clean energy solutions will limit growth, reduce jobs, and even threaten the viability of their business models.

Proponents of climate action, on the other hand, have emphasized the economic opportunities associated with green reform plans like the Green New Deal and President Biden's Build Back Better initiative. Clean energy technology is one of the fastest-growing sectors of the economy, exhibiting nearly double the growth rate of the economy as a whole over the past several years. And emerging green jobs often come with better pay and a safer work environment than many jobs in the traditional industrial sectors.

One area of particular concern involves the skills and education requirements that workers will need to meet in order to compete for green jobs. Green jobs typically require a different (and often more intensive) educational background than many traditional industrial jobs. As a result, workers without a college degree or specific technical training will likely be at a disadvantage in a greener job market. But green policy advocates have proposed a number of measures to help mitigate these challenges, including new worker training programs and public initiatives to identify areas where green job growth is likely to be strongest. Additionally, large numbers of workers already perform green tasks in the course of jobs that are not typically identified as green. This type of indirect training will help to prepare such workers for the transition to a green job or career.

The viewpoints in this chapter examine the impact of climate and environmental policy on the job market from a variety of different angles. What emerges is a complex landscape of opportunities and challenges, both for workers and for the public policy officials responsible for designing policies to manage the transition toward a green economic future.

VIEWPOINT 1

> "Clean energy is already proving to be a larger job creation engine than the heavily subsidized fossil-fuels sector, putting Americans back to work in a lackluster economy."

The Green-Collar Economy Is Booming

Christina DiPasquale and Kate Gordon

In the following viewpoint, Christina DiPasquale and Kate Gordon cite a number of data points and economic analyses to demonstrate why a general optimism about the future of green jobs is justified. DiPasquale and Gordon examine current employment numbers and future projections for new jobs in various sectors of the green economy and conclude that green jobs are not only vital to the current economy but likely to expand dramatically in the decades to come. Christina DiPasquale is founder and CEO of the progressive communications firm Balestra Media. Kate Gordon is an economist and senior policy adviser at the US Department of Energy.

"Top 10 Reasons Why Green Jobs Are Vital to Our Economy," by Christina DiPasquale and Kate Gordon, Center for American Progress, September 7, 2011. Reprinted by permission.

Are the Potential Benefits of the Green Economy Worth the Risks?

As you read, consider the following questions:

1. How can green jobs enhance America's competitive position in the global economy?
2. Which sectors of the green economy are likely to produce significant numbers of new green jobs in the next few years?
3. How can public policy measures encourage the creation of new green jobs?

Green jobs are integral to any effort to jumpstart our economy and reduce as rapidly as possible our 9.1 percent unemployment rate. The rapid growth of green jobs will boost demand in our economy by reducing unemployment, make America more competitive in the global economy, and protect our public health—all of which will result in greater economic productivity and long-term economic prosperity. Here are the top 10 reasons why this is the case today and into the future:

1. There are already 2.7 million jobs across the clean economy. Clean energy is already proving to be a larger job creation engine than the heavily subsidized fossil-fuels sector, putting Americans back to work in a lackluster economy.
2. Across a range of clean energy projects, including renewable energy, transit, and energy efficiency, for every million dollars spent, 16.7 green jobs are created. That is over three times the 5.3 jobs per million dollars that are created from the same spending on fossil-fuel industries.
3. The clean energy sector is growing at a rate of 8.3 percent. Solar thermal energy expanded by 18.4 percent annually from 2003 to 2010, along with solar photovoltaic power by 10.7 percent, and biofuels by 8.9 percent over the same period. Meanwhile, the U.S. wind energy industry saw 35 percent average annual growth over the past five years, accounting for 35 percent of new U.S. power capacity in

that period, according to the 2010 U.S. Wind Industry Annual Market Report. As a whole, the clean energy sector's average growth rate of 8.3 percent annually during this period was nearly double the growth rate of the overall economy during that time.

4. The production of cleaner cars and trucks is employing over 150,000 workers across the United States today. These job numbers are likely to increase as improved car and light truck standards recently announced by President Barack Obama will require more skilled employees and encourage further investment.

5. Median wages are 13 percent higher in green energy careers than the economy average. Median salaries for green jobs are $46,343, or about $7,727 more than the median wages across the broader economy. As an added benefit, nearly half of these jobs employ workers with a less than a four-year college degree, which accounts for a full 70 percent of our workforce.

6. Green jobs are made in America, spurring innovation with more U.S. content than other industries. Most of the products used in energy efficiency retrofits are more than 90 percent made in America. Sheet metal for ductwork is over 99 percent domestically sourced, as are vinyl windows (98 percent) and rigid foam insulation (more than 95 percent). Even major mechanical equipment such as furnaces (94 percent) and air conditioning and heat pumps (82 percent) are predominantly American made.

7. We have a positive trade balance in solar power components such as photovoltaic components and solar heating and cooling components of $1.9 billion, and are exporting components to China. Contrast this with the oil industry, where in 2010 alone we imported over $250 billion in petroleum-related products. As our nation's basic manufacturing base declines, we risk losing our place in

24 Million New Jobs

A shift to a greener economy could create 24 million new jobs globally by 2030 if the right policies are put in place, says the International Labour Organization (ILO).

According to the ILO's new report, the World Employment and Social Outlook, the new jobs will be created by adopting sustainable practices in the energy sector, using electric vehicles, and increasing energy efficiency in existing and future buildings.

The report refutes assertions that greening the economy will result in job losses and economic deterioration.

"The green economy can enable millions more people to overcome poverty and deliver improved livelihoods for this and future generations." ILO Deputy Director-General Deborah Greenfield said, adding that "This is a very positive message of opportunity in a world of complex choices."

As the world moves to a greener economy, an estimated 6 million jobs will be lost, including in the areas of petroleum extraction and refinery, coal mining and production of electricity from coal. To offset this, the report states that complementary policies will be needed to protect workers and ensure that the transition is just, the same report shows.

ILO suggests that well-designed policies could strengthen social protection and support green investment that is financially viable and conducive to higher growth; that leads to employment creation and fairer income distribution. However, policy creation is not the only answer for just transition. It will also require stronger commitment by firms to achieve environmental sustainability at the global level.

Globally, 1.2 billion jobs depend on a stable and healthy environment. Industries like agriculture, fisheries and forestry, as well as tourism and pharmaceuticals, depend on natural environmental processes.

Projected temperature increases and environmental degradation hurts jobs and working conditions, as work depends on natural resources, on ecosystem services and on a stable, disaster-free environment. In fact, ILO predicts that 72 million full-time jobs will be lost by 2030 due to heat stress, and temperature increases will lead to shorter available work hours, particularly in agriculture.

"Green Economy Could Create 24 Million New Jobs," United Nations, April 3, 2019.

the forefront of innovation if we don't invest in advanced manufacturing in the green sector.
8. Three separate programs for energy efficiency retrofits have employed almost 25,000 Americans in three months. The Weatherization Assistance Program, Energy Efficiency Block Grant Program, and State Energy Programs have collectively upgraded over half a million buildings since the programs began to ramp up from April 1, 2011, and June 30, 2011, providing immediate new and sustainable job opportunities to tens of thousands of construction workers eagerly searching for work.
9. Clean energy jobs are better for U.S. small businesses. Specialty construction companies that perform energy retrofits show very high rates of small business participation in the construction. Ninety-one percent of the firms involved in retrofits are small businesses with less than 20 employees.
10. An abundance of jobs in the green sector are manufacturing jobs with an upward career track. Forty-one percent of the nation's green jobs offer medium to long-term career building and training opportunities, and 26 percent of green jobs are in the manufacturing sector, compared to 9 percent in the traditional economy.

The bottom line: Green jobs being created through smart investments in our energy infrastructure are expanding employment opportunities while reducing pollution of our air and water, providing an alternative to foreign oil, and allowing us to export more American-made goods abroad.

VIEWPOINT

> *"Politicians focus on the tangible, seen benefits of their proposed spending, but they routinely overlook, downplay, and deny the unseen costs of such projects."*

The Bipartisan Infrastructure Bill Won't Create Jobs as Advertised

Brad Polumbo

In the following viewpoint, Brad Polumbo argues that President Biden's bipartisan infrastructure bill, which was passed and signed into law after this viewpoint was written, might indeed fulfill many of its promises. However, he contends, the promise that the government spending plan would create millions of jobs was misleading. The author cites a Wharton Business School analysis that projects the plan would yield a net zero effect on employment and economic growth. Brad Polumbo is a libertarian-conservative journalist and policy correspondent at the Foundation for Economic Education.

As you read, consider the following questions:

1. How much is the bipartisan infrastructure bill?
2. What are net jobs?
3. Is job creation the only focus of the infrastructure legislation?

"An Ivy League Analysis Just Destroyed Biden's Biggest Argument for the Bipartisan Infrastructure Bill," by Brad Polumbo, Foundation for Economic Education, August 9, 2021. https://fee.org/articles/an-ivy-league-analysis-just-destroyed-bidens-biggest-argument-for-the-bipartisan-infrastructure-bill/. Licensed under CC BY-4.0 International.

The bipartisan infrastructure legislation moving through Congress could end up on President Biden's desk before we know it. The $1 trillion bill has reportedly cleared major hurdles in the Senate and will soon land before the House of Representatives. The president would almost certainly sign the bill, which has his support, and its bipartisan passage would represent a political victory for the Biden administration.

At least, at first.

The promised long-term economic benefits from the sweeping $1 trillion expenditure will likely never materialize, according to a new Ivy League analysis. This runs directly against the president's promises that it would create jobs and stimulate the economy. Indeed, Biden has insisted that the government spending plan will "create millions of good-paying jobs."

"This bill makes key investments to put people to work all across the country," the president said. "It's going to put Americans to work in good-paying union jobs building and repairing our roads, bridges, ports, airports."

He additionally claimed that the plan is a "blue-collar blueprint" for economic opportunity because, supposedly, 90 percent of the jobs created "will not require a college degree."

This rhetoric is likely to appeal to many Americans. But the aforementioned analysis, by the Wharton Business School, pours cold water on the president's rosy promises. In stark contrast to "millions" of good jobs created, the Ivy League analysts project that the plan would have a net zero effect on employment, wages, and economic growth over both the medium-term (by 2031) and the long-term (by 2050).

Despite these meager results, the legislation would still add a whopping $351 billion to the national debt. For context, that's roughly $2,449 in new debt per federal taxpayer.

Well, as the analysts explain, it would indeed create some jobs via public works investment. This is what Biden and other advocates focus on. But there are also significant costs, since the resources invested in government infrastructure spending are ultimately not going toward private-sector investments that would otherwise have occurred. When the Wharton analysts compared the outcomes with these costs in mind, they found no actual net benefit.

This revealing analysis reminds us of the timeless principle explained by Henry Hazlitt in his classic work *Economics in One Lesson*. The scholar explained why public works schemes are not inherently the job-creating programs that politicians claim.

The politicians, like Biden in this case, focus on the tangible, seen benefits of their proposed spending, like the infrastructure jobs created. But they routinely overlook, downplay, and deny the unseen costs of such projects, misleading the public by only presenting them with half of the cost-benefit analysis. Hazlitt aptly explained this phenomenon with the example of a government bridge-building program.

"For every public job created by the bridge project a private job has been destroyed somewhere else," he wrote. "We can see the men employed on the bridge. We can watch them at work. The employment argument of the government spenders becomes vivid, and probably for most people convincing. But there are other things that we do not see, because, alas, they have never been permitted to come into existence."

"They are the jobs destroyed by the [money] taken from the taxpayers," Hazlitt continues. "All that has happened, at best, is that there has been a diversion of jobs because of the project. More bridge builders; fewer automobile workers, radio technicians, clothing workers, farmers."

Of course, this debate over job creation exists as just one part of the infrastructure debate. Biden is still free to argue that his proposed spending is otherwise necessary. But modern Ivy League analysis and timeless economic principles alike debunk the president's argument that the bipartisan infrastructure bill will create millions of jobs.

VIEWPOINT

> *"The most valued skills in the American workplace fall into the category of 'fundamental skills.'"*

There Is a Demand for Analytical Skills in a Green Job Market

Rakesh Kochhar

In the following viewpoint, Rakesh Kochhar examines how skill requirements for new and emerging green jobs differ from those in the industrial job economy. Using data from the US government's Occupational Information Network (O*NET), he compares the demand for mechanical and analytic skills in different areas of the economy, particularly in new industries that involve green technologies. He concludes by identifying a number of fundamental skills that will be critical for workers in the green economy. Rakesh Kochhar is an economist and senior researcher at the Pew Research Center.

As you read, consider the following questions:

1. How do skills for traditional jobs and green jobs differ?
2. What is the most valuable skill set in the contemporary US job economy?
3. Which mechanical skills are likely to be most valuable in the green economy?

"New, Emerging Jobs and the Green Economy Are Boosting Demand for Analytical Skills," by Rakesh Kochhar, Pew Research Center, March 23, 2020.

Are the Potential Benefits of the Green Economy Worth the Risks?

In a changing U.S. labor market, new and emerging occupations—including those that are linked to a green economy or the adoption of newer technologies—are raising the importance of analytical skills, such as science, mathematics and programming, according to a new Pew Research Center analysis of federal government job-skills data.

New and emerging occupations either represent new lines of work or are newly deserving of their own classification due to rising employment and other factors. Examples of novel jobs include database architects and informatics nurse specialists. Among newly classified occupations are biostatisticians and intelligence analysts.

But the green economy is also raising the demand for some mechanical skills, such as equipment maintenance and repairing, which have diminished in importance in recent decades as the number of U.S. manufacturing jobs declines. With its emphasis on the environment and the sustainable use of resources, the green economy has stimulated employment in existing engineering and production jobs, ranging from industrial engineers to electricians, which often call for mechanical proficiency.

Amid these changes, the most valued skills in the American workplace fall into the category of "fundamental skills"—active listening, speaking, critical thinking and reading comprehension. The skill that is currently most in demand among employers is active listening, or the ability to give full attention, take the time to understand, ask questions and not interrupt at inopportune times.

The most significant difference between newer and older occupations is in the importance for analytical skills. Several newer occupations, such as web administrators and data warehousing specialists, have a great need for programming skills. As a result, the average importance rating for programming skills in newer occupations is 34% higher than the average rating in older occupations, 2.03 vs. 1.52—among the biggest contrasts between the two groups of occupations, according to our analysis of data from the government's Occupational Information Network (O*NET).

(O*NET assesses the importance of 35 job skills on a scale of one, not important, to five, extremely important. Among the 967 occupations listed in the O*NET, some 147 are classified as "new and emerging.")

Other newer occupations, such as energy engineers and nanosystems engineers, are more intensive users of scientific expertise, boosting the importance rating for science in newer occupations to an average of 2.52, compared with 1.89 among older occupations. Also, the average importance of systems evaluation, a key skill for supply chain managers, is 23% higher among newer occupations, as is the rating for systems analysis, valuable for logistics engineers.

The need for mathematics, a critical skill in newer occupations such as biostatisticians and financial quantitative analysts, is also on the rise. The average rating of mathematics among newer occupations is 2.97 ("important" on the O*NET scale), compared with 2.48 among older occupations. Other skills in greater demand among newer occupations include writing, reading comprehension and critical thinking.

The Green Economy Needs More Analytical and Mechanical Skills

A key feature of the modern-day economy is the focus on activities devoted to curbing pollution and greenhouse gas emissions, economizing on fossil fuels and using more renewable sources, increasing energy efficiency, and recycling. Collectively labeled the "green economy," these activities give birth to new lines of work. They also either raise the demand for workers in existing occupations or change the skill requirements of some occupations.

Presently, the O*NET classifies 199 occupations as "green occupations." Seventy-one of these occupations are classified as "new and emerging"—such as biofuels production managers, solar energy systems engineers and climate change analysts. Like newer occupations overall, green economy occupations that are newer also require greater proficiency in analytical skills. Compared with older occupations, the average importance of programming and science skills is at least 34% higher among newer green economy occupations, and the average importance of mathematics, systems analysis and system evaluation is at least 25% higher.

Some green occupations call for greater proficiency in mechanical skills compared with older occupations. These 64 occupations are not new, and neither have they transformed as a result of the needs of the green economy. However, the demand for workers in these occupations, such as industrial engineers and hydrologists, is on the rise due to the emergence of the green economy.

Older green jobs are significantly more likely to require greater proficiency in the following mechanical skills: repairing, equipment maintenance, operation and control, troubleshooting and equipment selection. Compared with older jobs overall, the average importance of these skills is higher by upwards of 22% in older green jobs that are in increased demand.

Our analysis estimates that the 199 occupations listed as "green occupations" in the O*NET, whether older or newer, employed from 31 million to 34 million workers in 2018. This represents about 21% to 24% of overall U.S. employment of 145 million in 2018. Green occupations also paid better than average in 2018: about $30 per hour compared with $25 per hour across all jobs, roughly 20% more as expressed in 2018 dollars.

Across All Jobs, Fundamental Skills Are Most in Need, Mechanical Skills the Least

Looking across the American workplace overall, the most valued skills are fundamental skills. Among the 35 skills evaluated in the O*NET, the top four are fundamental in nature—active listening, speaking, critical thinking and reading comprehension. Rounding off the list of the top five skills is monitoring, a social skill pertaining to the assessment of performance in order to make improvements.

Active listening had an importance rating of 3.6 in 2020, averaged across all occupations, on a scale of one to five. It was rated "very important" to "extremely important" in 270 occupations, such as mental health counselors, and at least "somewhat important" in all occupations. There is no occupation in 2020 in which active listening is "not important"; it is a ubiquitous skill. A similar combination of high importance ratings and prevalent need propels other fundamental skills to the top of the skills ladder.

The bottom rung of the skills ladder in the labor market features a cluster of mechanical skills, namely equipment selection, equipment maintenance, repairing and installation. These skills may be extremely important in some occupations, but they are not in widespread use. For example, installation is extremely important for solar thermal installers and technicians, but it rates important or higher in only 22 occupations.

Programming, an analytical skill, also appears on the lowest rung. Although it is a higher-order computer skill in demand in newer jobs, it is in limited use in the labor market overall. There are only five occupations, including computer programmers, in which programming rates very important to extremely important in 2020. On the other hand, programming is rated not important in 163 occupations. In between the five highest and lowest rated skills are a mix of other fundamental skills, social skills, analytical skills, managerial skills and mechanical skills. Social skills cluster near the top of the skills ratings, with six of seven social skills ranked among the 15 most highly rated skills. Most analytical skills rank among the 15 lowest rated skills, on average.

Even as newer and greener occupations prioritize analytical skills and revive the need for mechanical skills in some cases, they share one essential trait with older occupations. Regardless of which group of occupations is examined, active listening, speaking, critical thinking and reading comprehension feature at the top of the list of skills ratings. In other words, preparation in fundamental skills remains the common currency in the workplace.

Viewpoint 4

> *"That's typical for most big-government environmental policies: they're so focused on prescriptive ways to control people's behaviors that they crowd out or ignore opportunities for innovative solutions."*

Green New Deal Legislation Is Bad for the Economy and the Environment

Nicolas Loris

In the following viewpoint, Nicolas Loris argues that the Green New Deal (GND) would not only fail to address the climate crisis in a useful way, but that it also would have a negative impact on the lives of most Americans. The author maintains that such policy would only serve to tighten government control over the private sector, yielding unintended consequences that will be worse, not better, for the environment. Nicolas Loris is an economist who focuses on energy and environmental and regulatory issues for the Heritage Foundation.

"It's Not Just About Cost. The Green New Deal Is Bad Environmental Policy, Too," by Nicolas Loris, The Heritage Foundation, November 15, 2019. Reprinted by permission.

As you read, consider the following questions:

1. How much would switching from fossil fuels to renewable energy cost, according to the viewpoint?
2. What unintended consequences might moving away from fracking have on many Americans?
3. Why does the author note the absence of nuclear plants in the GND's plans?

We're not hearing much about the "Green New Deal" these days, but it's still a priority for some candidates, as anyone who's attended a recent Bernie Sanders rally can attest.

Criticism of the GND tends to center on cost and rightly so. It would be extremely expensive. Researchers estimate it would take more than $5 trillion just to switch from coal, nuclear and natural gas to 100% renewables.

But even if you set economic concerns aside, an ironic fact remains: In the United States and around the world, the central-planning policies at the heart of the GND have a horrible track record for the environment.

Governments in countries such as Venezuela and China (or in the past like the Soviet Union and Cuba) either routinely mismanage and waste resources, or ramp up production with little to no accountability for environmental damage that comes with it. The absence of price signals reduces the incentive to be more efficient and do more with less.

In addition, the absence of property rights reduces the incentive to conserve and gives government-controlled industries a free pass to pollute without compensating or protecting its citizens.

The Green New Deal would massively expand the size and scope of the federal government's control over activities best left to the private sector. It would empower the feds to change and control how people produce and consume energy, harvest crops, raise livestock, build homes, drive cars and manufacture goods.

Secondly, the Green New Deal would result in a number of unintended consequences. For instance, policies that limit coal, oil and natural gas production in the United States will not stop the global consumption of these natural resources. Production will merely shift to places where the environmental standards are not as rigorous, making the planet worse off.

Moreover, it's not as if wind, solar and battery technologies magically appear. Companies still have to mine the resources, manufacture the product and deal with the waste streams. There are challenges to disposing potentially toxic lithium-ion batteries and solar panels, or even wind turbine blades that are difficult and expensive to transport and crush at landfills. While these are solvable problems, they're seldom discussed by GND proponents.

There would also be massive land use changes required to expand renewable power. Ben Zycher at the American Enterprise Institute estimates that land use necessary to meet a 100% renewable target would require 115 million acres, which is 15% larger than the land area of California.

Two recent National Bureau of Economic Research papers underscore the unintended consequences of energy policy on human well-being. One found that cheaper home heating because of America's fracking revolution is averting more than 10,000 winter deaths per year. The Green New Deal would wipe all of that away, and reverse course by mandating pricier energy on families.

Another paper found that the Japanese government's decision to close safely operating nuclear power plants after Fukashima increased energy prices and reduced consumption, which consequently, increased mortalities from colder temperatures. In fact, the authors estimate that "the decision to cease nuclear production has contributed to more deaths than the accident itself." Unintended consequences.

Another hallmark of bad environmental policy is focusing on outputs, not outcomes. According to the frequently asked questions sheet released along with the Green New Deal, it is "a massive investment in renewable energy production and would not include creating new nuclear plants."

One would think that if we only have 11 or 12 years to act on climate change, we'd want to grab the largest source of emissions-free electricity we can get. But that's not the case.

That's typical for most big-government environmental policies: they're so focused on prescriptive ways to control people's behaviors that they crowd out or ignore opportunities for innovative solutions.

The reality is that environmental policies aren't good for the environment if they're so bad for people. The costs of the GND would be devastatingly high for households. Government policies that drive up energy bills are not only very regressive, but they would also harm consumers multiple times as they pay more for food, clothes and all of the other goods that require energy to make.

By shrinking our economy by potentially tens of trillions of dollars, the Green New Deal will cause lower levels of prosperity and fewer resources to deal with whatever environmental challenges come our way. That's a bad deal for our economy and our environment.

VIEWPOINT 5

> "44.3% of U.S. workers already have the transferable skills needed to contribute to the green economy."

How Many Green Jobs Are There in the US?
Karlygash Kuralbayeva

In the following viewpoint, Karlygash Kuralbayeva analyzes the landscape of green jobs and what she calls "indirect" green jobs. She examines the percentage of jobs that currently qualify as green and also a number of areas where jobs involve specific green tasks. She argues that the transition to a green economy may be easier than anticipated because workers who currently perform green tasks in their jobs are likely to be well-prepared for the fully green jobs of the future. Karlygash Kuralbayeva is a lecturer in the department of political economy at Kings College London. She specializes in research on the economics of climate change and environmental policy.

As you read, consider the following questions:

1. What qualifies as a "green" job?
2. What is an "indirect" green job?
3. Why is the transition to a green economy likely to be easier for workers than the transition to a computerized, IT-driven economy was?

"How Many Green Jobs Are There in the US?" by Karlygash Kuralbayeva, London School of Economics, May 9, 2018. Reprinted by permission.

According to a new report from the International Renewable Energy Agency there are 10.3 million renewable energy jobs globally—a 5.3% increase since 2017. The latest report on the makeup of the U.S. energy sector workforce also revealed that renewable energy employment is growing. During 2016, the U.S. solar workforce increased by 25% and the number of employees in the U.S. wind energy industry increased by 32%.

Whilst these reports indicate that the number of employees in green jobs is growing they look at only at the energy and electricity-generation sectors. In the U.S. the electricity-generation sector is relatively small at around 5% of the total workforce.

In our latest research we used data on the U.S. job market to estimate how many green jobs there are in the rest of the U.S. workforce and, for those jobs which are not green, how the transition to a low-carbon economy could affect them.

1 in 10 U.S. Workers Already Carry Out Green Tasks in Their Jobs

The U.S. Bureau of Labour Statistics (BLS) estimate that in 2011 2.6% of the U.S. workforce were employed in the production of green goods and services. These jobs reduce fossil fuel usage, decrease pollution and greenhouse gas emissions, involve recycling materials, increasing energy efficiency or the development of renewable energy sources.

However, in our recent paper in the journal *Energy Economics*, we estimated that the actual number of people in jobs already supporting the green economy could be much higher.

Using data from BLS from 2014 and from the U.S. Department of Labour's Occupational Network Database (O*NET) we found that there is a spectrum of green jobs. Most estimates of green jobs only include occupations that are unique to the green economy, for example wind turbine service technicians or solar photovoltaic installers. When we looked at the O*NET data we found that there are many occupations that involve some green tasks but are sometimes excluded from estimates of green jobs.

We found in our analysis that 1.2% of U.S. jobs are unique to the green economy. On average, 59.4% of the tasks involved in these jobs are "green tasks" as defined by data we used from the O*NET dataset, which looks at the types of tasks involved in 858 (out of 974) U.S. occupations and how often the tasks are carried out.

An additional 9.1% of the workforce are doing green tasks in their jobs but less often, for example workers who are urban and regional planners or refuse and recyclable material collectors. On average, 30.4% of the tasks carried out in these jobs are green.

When we included all jobs in which workers are currently undertaking at least one green task per year we estimate that 10.3% of current U.S. jobs are "green."

What Proportion of the U.S. Workforce Is Green?

Our analysis highlights that a further 9.1% of the U.S. workforce are in jobs that will be necessary to support the green economy but which do not directly support green tasks. We call these "indirectly green jobs."

For example, financial analysts might forecast or analyse financial costs of climate change, identify environmentally-sound financial investments, and recommend environmentally-related financial products. These jobs do the behind-the-scenes work that contributes to green economic activity.

It is not easy to say how many of the workers in this category are currently supporting the green economy. However, we can say that these workers should be able to transition to working in jobs that support the green economy with little retraining since they will not need any new skills.

How Much Retraining Will the Rest of the Workforce Need to Work in the Green Economy?

The retraining needed for many workers to work in the green economy could be much more limited than expected.

Our analysis showed that another 44.3% of U.S. workers already have the transferable skills needed to contribute to the green economy. With limited retraining they could take up indirectly green work. For instance, retail workers could transition to work in retail for green products (for example, solar panels, or sustainably produced goods) and coal workers could transition to jobs in the solar photovoltaic industry due to overlapping skills.

This type of job movement could fuel a rapid increase in the workforce to support the green economy. In the longer term the "greening" of the labour market will require transitions to directly green jobs that are unique to the green economy (e.g., environmental engineer, recycling operator) which represent a wider skills gap and may require specific training.

And of course there are jobs that will not be affected by the low-carbon transition. 36.3 % of U.S. jobs, for example doctors and teachers, will remain the same after the low-carbon transition.

The "Greening" of the U.S. Labour Market Will Be Less Disruptive Than the IT Revolution

The labour market will change as the U.S. economy becomes greener, and the changes could be broad. In the late 1980s the labour market underwent another significant shift during the IT revolution. Studies have shown that information and communication technologies accounted for up to a quarter of the growth in demand for highly educated workers during the period 1980 and 2004 across eleven developed countries. Our analysis indicates that while some retraining is needed, the greening of the workforce in the U.S. will not be as disruptive as the changes under the IT revolution.

There is lots of potential for growth in the green workforce if career moves are strategically managed. Some ideas might be to encourage people planning a job change to apply for green jobs. Employers could help workers get experience of green work environments through job rotation or collaboration with green workers. This could help them learn to use their existing skills in a new way.

Periodical and Internet Sources Bibliography

The following articles have been selected to supplement the diverse views presented in this chapter.

Matt Egan, "Coal Miners Union Backs Biden's $2T Infrastructure Plan," CNN Business, April 20, 2021, https://www.cnn.com/2021/04/20/business/coal-union-biden-infrastructure/index.html.

Juliet Eilperin and Eli Rosenberg, "Biden's Wooing Both Labor and Environmentalists on Climate Change. Oil Pipelines May Drive Them Apart," *Washington Post*, May 7, 2021, https://www.washingtonpost.com/climate-environment/2021/03/07/biden-climate-change-unions-environment.

Roger Harrabin, "COP26: Leaders Agree to Global Plan to Boost Green Technology," BBC News, November 2, 2021, https://www.bbc.com/news/science-environment-59138622.

Anna Markova, "Want to Know What a Just Transition to a Green Economy Looks Like? Ask the Workers," *The Guardian*, October 18, 2021, https://www.theguardian.com/commentisfree/2021/oct/18/just-transition-green-economy-workers-resources-empowerment.

Sarah O'Connor, "Not All Green Jobs Are Safe and Clean," *Financial Times*, October 25, 2021, https://www.ft.com/content/111f9600-f440-47fb-882f-4a5e3c96fae2.

Noam Scheiber, "Building Solar Farms May Not Build the Middle Class," *New York Times*, July 16, 2021, https://www.nytimes.com/2021/07/16/business/economy/green-energy-jobs-economy.html.

Morgan Smith, "The 10 Most In-Demand Green Jobs Right Now—Some Pay Over $100,000 a year," CNBC, October 19, 2021, https://www.cnbc.com/2021/10/19/the-10-most-in-demand-green-jobs-right-now.html.

Jonathan Wilson, "Government Must Do More to Support the Skills Needed for Net Zero," *Engineering and Technology*, October 25, 2021, https://eandt.theiet.org/content/articles/2021/10/government-not-sufficiently-grappling-skills-gap-needed-for-net-zero-report-warns.

OPPOSING VIEWPOINTS® SERIES

CHAPTER 2

Can the US Afford to Improve Its Infrastructure with a Green Economy?

Chapter Preface

President Biden's Build Back Better plan is designed to accomplish several different goals at the same time. Two of the most important objectives are (1) to rebuild, repair, and modernize infrastructure systems across the United States and (2) to support the development and deployment of green technologies that will help to mitigate the effects of climate change. Climate activists have applauded the Build Back Better initiative, but a number of economists, business experts, and political pundits have questioned the overall cost of Biden's plan. Regardless of how the surrounding debate unfolds, green reform and infrastructure development are likely to remain near the center of the stage in US politics for the foreseeable future.

There is widespread agreement that the US infrastructure system—including roads and highways, power distribution networks, water delivery systems, etc.—is badly in need of an upgrade. Much of our infrastructure was designed and constructed decades ago, well before the policymakers or the general public were aware of climate change and other environmental hazards associated with industrial activity and urban development. But widespread agreement about the need for an upgrade has not produced a consensus about what steps should be taken or how to pay for them.

The foremost concern for many critics of green reform centers on the projected overall cost of plans like the Green New Deal and Build Back Better. Some of these critics worry about the adverse economic effects of raising taxes while others focus more on the risks associated with adding to the national debt. Even strong supporters of green reform have questioned the wisdom of financing green policies with deficit spending. The economist Edward Barbier, a founding member of the green movement in America, writes:

Saddling future generations of Americans with unsustainable levels of national debt is just as dangerous as burdening them with an economy that is environmentally unsustainable. Deficit spending is warranted to boost overall demand for goods and services when unemployment rises, consumers do not spend and private investment is down. When that is not the case, I believe efforts to grow green sectors should pay for themselves.[1]

But generally speaking, green reform advocates argue that the cost of inaction in the future will inevitably surpass the short-term costs associated with green reform. The viewpoint authors in this chapter represent a variety of perspectives on the economic impact of green reform and its associated costs.

Notes

1. America Can Afford a Green New Deal—Here's How," by Edward Barbier, The Conversation, February 26, 2019, https://theconversation.com/america-can-afford-a-green-new-deal-heres-how-111681. Licensed under CC BY-ND-4.0 International.

VIEWPOINT 1

> "The Green New Deal as proposed by Ocasio-Cortez and Markey would be expensive. But what policies are adopted and how we choose to pay for it could ultimately determine the plan's success and whether we can afford it."

The Overall Cost of Green Reform Matters Less Than How We Pay for It

Edward Barbier

In the following viewpoint, Edward Barbier argues that debates about the overall cost of climate and environmental policy initiatives like the Green New Deal are missing the point. From his perspective, the effectiveness of specific policies and the plans to pay for them are far more important than the top-line sticker price of any plan. Edward Barbier is a professor in the Department of Economics at Colorado State University, senior scholar at the School of Global Environmental Sustainability, and author/editor of more than 25 books. His work focuses on environmental and resource economics and he has consulted with the UN, the OECD, the World Bank, and a variety of NGOs.

"America Can Afford a Green New Deal—Here's How," by Edward Barbier, The Conversation, February 26, 2019, https://theconversation.com/america-can-afford-a-green-new-deal-heres-how-111681. Licensed under CC BY-ND-4.0 International.

As you read, consider the following questions:

1. Why does Barbier believe that green reform plans should avoid relying on deficit spending?
2. How might the impact of specific policies included within the Green New Deal help to lower the total cost of the plan over time?
3. According to the author, what are some of the benefits involved with using a carbon tax to help pay for green reform?

U.S. Rep. Alexandria Ocasio-Cortez and Sen. Ed Markey are calling for a "Green New Deal" that would involve massive government spending to shift the U.S. economy away from its reliance on carbon.

Their congressional resolution goes into great detail about the harms of climate change and what the U.S. government should do about it. Left unanswered, however, is how America would pay for it.

Some commentators have been calling a Green New Deal unaffordable, with some estimates putting the bill for complete decarbonization at as high as US$12.3 trillion.

As the author of the United Nations Environment Program's Global Green New Deal—a plan to lift the world economy out of the 2008-2009 Great Recession—I disagree. I believe there are two straightforward ways to cover the cost and help accelerate the green revolution, while lowering the overall price tag.

What a Green New Deal May Cost

Before we talk about how to pay for it, first we need a rough idea of how much it might actually cost.

For starters, it's important to be realistic. Rather than putting a price tag on going 100 percent renewable—which would take decades—I believe we should figure out how much to spend over the next five years to build a greener economy.

Ambitious efforts to foster green energy during the Great Recession are a good place to start.

In total, the world's largest 20 economies and a few others spent $3.3 trillion to stimulate economic growth. Of that, more than $520 billion was devoted to "green investments," such as pollution cleanup, recycling and low-carbon energy.

The U.S. share of that was about $120 billion, or about 1 percent of its gross domestic product. Around half of this went toward energy conservation and other short-term energy efficiency investments to quickly shore up the then-nascent recovery and generate employment.

The stimulus may have spurred some growth in renewable energy but didn't do much on its own to reduce carbon emissions permanently.

Another country that made fairly big green investments during the Great Recession was South Korea, which promoted "low carbon, green growth" as its new long-term development vision. It allocated $60 billion, or 5 percent of its 2007 GDP, to a five-year plan.

But in the end, South Korea may have spent only $26 billion on low-carbon energy and failed to adopt pricing reforms and other incentives to foster renewables, such as phasing out fossil fuel subsidies, pricing carbon and improving regulatory frameworks. The result was only a modest improvement in energy efficiency, and carbon emissions have continued to rise.

In other words, the price tag of a Green New Deal that would make a difference would have to be much higher than what governments like the U.S. and Korea actually spent during the Great Recession. The original South Korea five-year plan, however, to spend 5 percent of GDP to me seems about right, as the best guess of the public investment needed to decarbonize a major economy through a green growth strategy.

So if we use Korea as a starting point, that means the U.S. would need to spend around $970 billion over the next five years, or $194 billion annually.

How to Pay for the Green New Deal

As for paying for it, the first thing to bear in mind is that in my view a Green New Deal should be covered by current rather than future revenue.

A common way for Congress to pay for the cost of a new program or stimulus is by deficit spending. So the U.S. borrows the money from investors and then eventually has to pay it back through taxes down the road.

With the federal deficit projected to reach $1 trillion in 2019, increasing it by several hundred billion more—even if for a good cause—is not a great idea. Ballooning deficits add to the national debt, which is already $21 trillion and counting.

Saddling future generations of Americans with unsustainable levels of national debt is just as dangerous as burdening them with an economy that is environmentally unsustainable. Deficit spending is warranted to boost overall demand for goods and services when unemployment rises, consumers do not spend and private investment is down. When that is not the case, I believe efforts to grow green sectors should pay for themselves.

So the U.S. would have to find new revenue sources to finance additional government support for clean energy research and development, greening infrastructure, smart transmission grids, public transport and other programs under any Green New Deal. Two of the main ways to do that would be by raising new revenues or finding savings elsewhere in the budget.

On the revenue side, I believe passing a carbon tax is one of the best ways to go. A $20 tax per metric ton of carbon that climbs over time at a pace slightly higher than inflation would raise around $96 billion in revenue each year—covering just under half the estimated cost. At the same time, it would reduce carbon emissions by 11.1 billion metric tons through 2030.

In other words, not only does it help raise money to pay for a transition to a green economy, a carbon tax also helps spur that very change.

In terms of savings, the removal of fossil fuel subsidies is a particularly appropriate target. Consumer subsidies for fossil fuels and producer subsidies for coal cost U.S. taxpayers nearly $9 billion a year. These subsidies could be shifted instead to cover some expenditures under a Green New Deal.

And again, doing this would accelerate the transition to cleaner energy.

So where might the other $89 billion come from?

One option is to simply impose a higher carbon tax. A $20 tax would put the U.S. roughly in the middle among countries that currently impose carbon taxes. But doubling it to $40 per ton would raise an additional $76 billion annually, or $172 billion in total, as well as reduce 17.5 billion metric tons of carbon by 2030.

Another idea is to raise taxes on the highest-earning Americans. For example, imposing a 70 percent tax on earnings of $10 million or more would bring in an addtional $72 billion a year.

Cost Savings

But it's also possible that the cost of decarbonizing the economy may fall over time.

For example, the drop in emissions accompanying the carbon tax should lower the price tag in a way that's hard to estimate today. The right policies and reforms would also help lower the costs.

In a sort of "chicken and egg" effect, as economists Ken Gillingham and James Stock have shown, green innovations spur demand, which leads to more innovation, all of which ultimately reduce costs. A good illustration is purchases of electric vehicles, which will stimulate demand for charging stations. Once installed, the stations will reduce the costs of running electric vehicles and further boost demand.

The Green New Deal as proposed by Ocasio-Cortez and Markey would be expensive. But what policies are adopted and how we choose to pay for it could ultimately determine the plan's success and whether we can afford it.

VIEWPOINT 2

> "A key advantage of carbon pricing is that it treats all emissions equally—no business or household is required to take on higher costs of reducing its last ton of CO_2 than another."

Carbon Pricing Should Play a Major Role in Green Reform

Grant Jacobsen and Carolyn Fischer

In the following viewpoint, Grant Jacobsen and Carolyn Fischer examine the economics and policy implications of carbon pricing and the benefits of including carbon pricing initiatives as part of a broader green reform plan like the Green New Deal. Particular areas of focus include the differences between a carbon tax and a cap-and-trade system, the advantages of carbon pricing over regulatory standards, and how carbon pricing initiatives can help to spur innovation in the private sector. Grant Jacobsen is associate professor of climate studies and director of the Master of Public Administration program at the University of Oregon. His research focuses on renewable energy, environmental policy, and carbon offsets. Carolyn Fischer is research manager for sustainability and infrastructure at the World Bank and a research fellow of the European Institute of Environmental Economics.

"The Green New Deal and the Future of Carbon Pricing," by Grant Jacobsen and Carolyn Fischer, John Wiley & Sons, Inc., June 2, 2021. https://onlinelibrary.wiley.com/doi/full/10.1002/pam.22313. Licensed under CC BY-4.0.

Can the US Afford to Improve Its Infrastructure with a Green Economy?

As you read, consider the following questions:

1. According to the authors, what are some of the key advantages of carbon pricing as part of an overall green reform policy?
2. Why do the authors believe that a well-designed climate policy can help to encourage innovation?
3. What does the viewpoint mean by the "distributional effects" of climate policy?

Climate change and the set of policies that are motivated by it have become one of the most salient issues in American society and politics. Survey evidence from 2020 indicates that 60 percent of Americans feel that climate change is a major threat to the United States and 52 percent believe that addressing climate change should be a top policy priority (Kennedy, 2020). Growing concern related to climate change, combined with the election of President Joe Biden and Democratic control of both chambers of Congress, suggest that the coming years may be a pivotal era for climate policy in the United States.

The elevated importance of climate change has coincided with new discussions about the way in which climate policy should be structured. For many years, policy debates focused directly on climate change have, in large part, involved enacting a price on carbon, which could be implemented either through a carbon tax or cap-and-trade system. Within the U.S., interest in a carbon price perhaps peaked in 2009 with the American Clean Energy and Security (ACES) Act of 2009 (i.e., "Waxman-Markey" bill), which included the creation of an emissions trading scheme. The bill passed the House but was never brought to a vote in the Senate.

Most recently, the policy focus has shifted toward the "Green New Deal." The Green New Deal (GND), as embodied through a nonbinding House resolution (H.Res.109; 116th Congress) sponsored by Rep. Alexandria Ocasio-Cortez and Sen. Ed Markey, is an aspirational plan calling for aggressive change throughout the economy related to mitigating climate change and addressing other societal problems, most notably economic inequality and systemic injustice. Carbon pricing is not mentioned in the resolution, which instead focuses on setting ambitious goals. Among other items, the resolution calls for 1) "meeting 100 percent of the power demand in the United States through clean, renewable, and zero-emission energy sources"; 2) "upgrading all existing buildings in the United States and building new buildings to achieve maximum energy efficiency, water efficiency, safety, affordability, comfort, and durability, including through electrification"; 3) "removing pollution and greenhouse gas emissions from manufacturing and industry as much as is technologically feasible"; and 4) "overhauling transportation systems in the United States to remove pollution and greenhouse gas emissions from the transportation sector as much as is technologically feasible." The focus of these goals on zero or technology-based thresholds, as well as the absence of carbon pricing within the resolution, indicates that carbon mitigation policies under a GND-approach would likely take place through regulatory mandates, such as standards for power production, energy efficiency, and transportation.

The relevance of the GND to recent discussions related to climate change is hard to overstate. It certainly has become more prominent than a carbon tax or cap-and-trade and more readily embraced by politicians. For example, Senator Bernie Sanders, who featured a carbon tax in his 2016 presidential campaign, eschewed a carbon price for a climate policy centered around the GND during his 2020 campaign. President Biden's administration has also embraced at least a modified version of the GND approach to climate policy and one of the leading candidates to head the EPA under the Biden Administration, Mary Nichols, was reportedly removed from consideration in part due to her previous support for carbon pricing in California (Davenport, 2020). These political trends are also reflected in the interest of the public. For example, Google Trends data, which capture Google search volumes for different topics reveal that carbon pricing experienced a surge in

The American Jobs Plan

While the American Rescue Plan is changing the course of the pandemic and delivering relief for working families, this is no time to build back to the way things were. This is the moment to reimagine and rebuild a new economy. The American Jobs Plan is an investment in America that will create millions of good jobs, rebuild our country's infrastructure, and position the United States to out-compete China. Public domestic investment as a share of the economy has fallen by more than 40 percent since the 1960s. The American Jobs Plan will invest in America in a way we have not invested since we built the interstate highways and won the Space Race.

The United States of America is the wealthiest country in the world, yet we rank 13th when it comes to the overall quality of our infrastructure. After decades of disinvestment, our roads, bridges, and water systems are crumbling. Our electric grid is vulnerable to catastrophic outages. Too many lack access to affordable, high-speed Internet and to quality housing. The past year has led to job losses and threatened economic security, eroding more than 30 years of progress in women's labor force participation. It has unmasked the fragility of our caregiving infrastructure. And, our nation is falling behind its biggest competitors on research and development (R&D), manufacturing, and training. It has never been more important for us to invest in strengthening our infrastructure and competitiveness, and in creating the good-paying, union jobs of the future.

Like great projects of the past, the President's plan will unify and mobilize the country to meet the great challenges of our time: the climate crisis and the ambitions of an autocratic China. It will invest in Americans and deliver the jobs and opportunities they deserve. But unlike past major investments, the plan prioritizes addressing long-standing and persistent racial injustice. The plan targets 40 percent of the benefits of climate and clean infrastructure investments to disadvantaged communities. And, the plan invests in rural communities and communities impacted by the market-based transition to clean energy.

"Fact Sheet: The American Jobs Plan," The White House, March 31, 2021.

interest around the time of the Waxman-Markey bill, but it has subsequently declined; meanwhile, interest in the GND surged in 2019 and remained elevated relative to carbon pricing in 2020.

A natural question now, given the trends outlined above, is whether the GND is a wise approach to climate policy. In this article, we discuss the future of U.S. climate policy within the context of the GND. The GND has many features, and this article is not meant to provide a comprehensive evaluation of all components of it. Rather, we focus on carbon pricing and whether it, rather than mandates and standards, should feature more centrally in the future of U.S. climate policy. We orient our discussion around issues related to theoretical aspects of different climate policy instruments and empirical evidence on their performance. We consider the efficiency and effectiveness of different approaches, their distributional aspects and how these relate to the increasingly important environmental justice priorities, and their political feasibility.

To preview our overall conclusions, we believe carbon pricing should play a role in the future of climate policy. When designed properly, carbon pricing has clear advantages over regulatory standards. While the historical performance of carbon pricing to date has been modest (as has the performance of regulatory standards), that is because most pricing schemes have been designed inadequately (e.g., with prices that are much too low). With respect to equity and environmental justice, existing evidence suggests that an appropriately designed carbon price would lead to better distributional outcomes than regulatory standards. Finally, we fail to find evidence that ambitious regulatory standards would be more politically acceptable than an ambitious carbon price.

The Economic Case for Carbon Pricing

The economic case for carbon pricing is well known among economists and policy wonks, although possibly less appreciated among the public. The High-Level Commission on Carbon Pricing led by Nobel prize-winning economist Joseph Stiglitz and Lord

Nicholas Stern stated prominently, "A well-designed carbon price is an indispensable part of a strategy for reducing emissions in an efficient way" (Carbon Pricing Leadership Coalition, 2017, p. 3). The reason is that carbon pricing activates incentives throughout the economy, all along the value chain, for taking the costs of emissions into account when making decisions, large and small, about energy use, production processes, technology investments, and consumption habits. No other instrument can do that, and no regulator can fathom standards for all the opportunities to reduce emissions and the ingenuity to develop new products and technologies.

A key advantage of carbon pricing is that it treats all emissions equally—no business or household is required to take on higher costs of reducing its last ton of CO_2 than another. Every actor is incentivized to reduce their emissions further as long as that is cheaper than paying the price, and this marginal cost equalization is a key component of cost-effectiveness that inflexible standards by definition lack. Furthermore, carbon pricing ensures that polluters pay for their emissions. By contrast, reliance on subsidies to low-carbon technologies imposes the burden on taxpayers and leverages only a narrow set of options to crowd out dirty sources.

Proponents of technology-based mandates often argue that guaranteed markets for these technologies are needed to drive scale economies and innovation. Of course, most demand-pull policies will drive innovation in improving and lowering the costs of those technologies that are demanded. However, carbon pricing can play an important role in creating expectations that there will be markets for new low-carbon products and technologies that standards and mandates, having to be more explicit about eligibility, have a hard time conceiving.

An ideal policy mix would supplement carbon pricing with policies that correct for market barriers and missing incentives for innovation and adoption of clean technologies, including support for R&D and de-risking investments. Done well, such complementary policies can certainly improve the cost-effectiveness of carbon pricing. However, done poorly, heavy-handed policies and excess reliance on specific technologies can double or triple the costs of achieving the desired emissions reductions, even taking all these additional market imperfections into account (Fischer, Preonas, & Newell, 2017). The reason is that the more specific the mandate or targeted subsidy, the fewer opportunities for emissions reductions that can be taken. For example, relying predominately on building out renewable energy neglects the considerable emissions reductions that can be achieved in the meantime by switching to lower-emitting fuels and energy conservation.

Empirical Evidence on Climate Policy and Carbon Mitigation

Carbon prices have been implemented, scheduled for implementation, or are under consideration in at least 61 jurisdictions, providing an opportunity to empirically evaluate how effective they are in practice. Best et al. (2020) evaluate national data on carbon emissions and carbon pricing and find that the average annual growth rate of carbon emissions from fuel combustion has been about two percentage points lower in countries with carbon prices. In a meta-analysis, Green (2021) presents related evidence that carbon pricing is associated with a zero to 2 percent reduction in emissions per year. These reductions are modest considering the emissions reductions targets that have been set under international agreements. Models indicate that CO_2 emissions must decline by about 45 percent from 2010 levels by 2030 to avoid global temperature change of greater than 1.5 degrees C (IPCC, 2018).

Ex post analyses using micro data further confirm significant effects of carbon pricing on emissions reductions and investments, without significant changes to employment or profits (Venmans et al., 2020). Studies comparing firms regulated by the European Union (EU) Emissions Trading System (ETS) to similar firms below the coverage threshold estimate that the carbon price caused covered firms to reduce their emissions by around 10 percent, despite an extended period of low prices (Martin, Muûls, & Wagner, 2016). Studies of the carbon tax in British Columbia found that its modest price, which rose gradually to about USD $22.20 by 2012, reduced emissions by 5 to 15 percent with negligible effects on the overall provincial economy (Murray & Rivers, 2015).

In addition to reducing emissions, a key aspect of any climate policy is that it leads to innovation. As with mitigating emissions, carbon pricing has been shown to be an effective tool for spurring innovation, although the magnitude of the effect has been modest. Calel and Dechezleprêtre (2016) find that EU ETS caused covered firms to increase their research effort, with their patent applications for clean technologies rising by 9 percent. Weak carbon prices, which occurred with the collapse of allowance values for several years in the EU ETS, diminished clean patenting activity (Bel & Joseph, 2018). Studies of other carbon pricing systems confirm that carbon prices encourage innovation, although primarily incrementally rather than through disruptive innovation (Grubb et al., 2021).

While carbon pricing does not have a strong record of creating large emissions reductions or breakthrough technologies, the primary reason for this is not the use of pricing itself, but the fact that carbon pricing schemes have been limited in scope and used prices that were beneath what would be required to achieve more aggressive reductions. Carbon prices in the range of $40 to $80 in 2020 are needed to reduce emissions in line with the goals of the Paris Agreement (Carbon Pricing Leadership Coalition, 2017). Until very recently, more than half of covered emissions have been under a carbon price of less than $10 and the global average carbon price is $2/t$CO_2$ (Parry, 2019). However, today EU ETS allowances are trading at the equivalent of nearly $50 and Canada has announced a carbon tax hike to reach CAD 170 (US $135) by 2030.

Does carbon pricing's modest historical effectiveness mean carbon prices cannot be more effective going forward? We remain optimistic about the potential use of carbon pricing for several reasons. First, market-based policies have been shown to perform well when designed appropriately. Schmalensee and Stavins (2013) review the performance of the SO_2 allowance trading program. During its first phase, before it was mostly rendered obsolete by changes in the broader regulatory environment, the program performed "exceptionally well along all relevant dimensions" and led to sharp reductions in emissions and substantial cost savings relative to what would have been accrued under a command-and-control regulatory approach. Secondly, gas taxes—which have similar properties to a carbon tax—have been shown to be effective at reducing gasoline consumption (Li et al., 2014). While the elasticity is modest, recent evidence suggests short-term gasoline elasticity demand may be greater than has been appreciated (Levin et al., 2017) and longer-run responsiveness would likely be even greater due to more time for adjustments to the vehicle fleet (Donna, 2019).

Moving forward, regardless of the choice of carbon policy, the key consideration is that the policy is designed with the features (e.g., the right carbon price) that are required to meet its objectives. As with carbon pricing, standards-based climate policies have not performed well when designed inadequately. For example, state renewable portfolio standards (RPS) appear to have created, on average, small or insignificant increases in renewable generation (Upton & Snyder, 2017) and the effect has depended on the design features of the RPS (Carley et al., 2017).

Climate Policy and Equity

Much of our discussion thus far has focused on the effect of carbon pricing on overall emissions levels. A critical issue for any climate policy is how it would affect different segments of society. Distributional effects, which have been somewhat neglected in historical discussions of climate policy, have become increasingly prominent in recent years and relate closely to the growing focus within society, policy, and academia on environmental justice.

A first-order question for environmental policies, including climate change policies, is how they alter the burden of pollution on different groups of society. This is an emerging empirical issue, but several recent studies provide new insights on how environmental policies alter the distribution of pollution. Hernandez-Cortes and Meng (2021) provide evidence that California's cap and trade system reversed previously widening "environmental justice gaps" in carbon co-pollutants, including particulate matter, NO_x, and SO_x. Similarly, Currie et al. (2019) provide evidence that the Clean Air Act was the single largest contributor to racial convergence in $PM_{2.5}$ since 2000.

This new evidence suggests that most varieties of environmental policies are likely to reduce disparities in environmental exposure to pollutants. Would a carbon price or regulatory standards approach lead to a greater reduction? The evidence along these lines is inconclusive, but recent investigations suggest it may not matter. Shapiro and Walker (2021) study how offset markets affect the dispersion of pollution in the context of the Clean Air Act. They conclude that "this analysis of 12 prominent offset markets suggest that they do not substantially increase or decrease the equity of environmental outcomes."

The distributional effects of any climate policy will go beyond their effects on pollution exposure, as they will have effects throughout the economy (e.g., effects on prices, wages, taxes, government spending, etc.). Green and Knittel (2020) present evidence on the projected distributional effect of carbon pricing based on census tract data and 12 different policy scenarios. Carbon pricing performs well from a distributional aspect here, too, especially when paired with a dividend to households. They conclude, "we find regulatory standards tend to be regressive and, on average, are a net cost to low-income households—especially those in rural areas. Carbon pricing, when accompanied with a dividend, is progressive for urban, rural, and suburban households, with the average low-income household receiving a larger dividend check than they spend in carbon taxes."

Climate Policy and Political Viability

Another important consideration for climate policy is whether it can be enacted politically. Perhaps the Green New Deal should avoid carbon pricing because pricing would imperil its viability? Mildenberger and Stokes (2020) argue along these lines, calling carbon pricing a "political disaster" based on experiences in Oregon, Australia, France, and elsewhere. However, focusing on the failures ignores the many political successes in other jurisdictions, including California, British Columbia, United Kingdom, Europe, and elsewhere. Given the scarce progress that the United States—and the globe—has made on enacting policies that would seriously limit carbon emissions, it might be more accurate to argue that enacting any form of climate policy that meaningfully limits emissions has been politically challenging.

The question then, moving forward, as the public's opinion on climate change appears to be trending toward greater climate concern, is which style of climate policy is most likely to succeed politically. In favor of carbon pricing, many jurisdictions have successfully implemented carbon pricing, so it is certainly feasible in some settings. As of 2020, 31 ETSs and 30 carbon taxes are in place or scheduled for implementation, covering about 22 percent of global greenhouse gas (GHG) emissions (World Bank Group, 2020). Indeed, the closest trade partners for the U.S.—Canada, Mexico, Europe, and even China—all have and are expanding their use of carbon pricing. Additionally, the revenue collected through carbon pricing can be helpful in making a policy more politically palatable—for example, it could be used to compensate industry for stranded assets, pay for popular subsidies to green investments and innovation, or minimize the net costs to lower income households. Finally, at least in theory, one could argue that the elevated cost-effectiveness of carbon pricing would make an ambitious climate policy politically acceptable.

Conclusion

We do not argue that a carbon price alone can achieve all the goals of the Green New Deal. However, a well-designed carbon price can certainly help achieve those goals, by 1) providing a direct incentive to reduce CO_2 emissions throughout the economy, 2) expanding demand for new clean technologies and innovations by ensuring they will be more competitive in the markets they serve, 3) raising revenues to pay for green investments and equity improvements the GND calls for, and 4) enabling greater ambition by lowering the overall cost of the clean energy transition. For these reasons, a Green New Deal would be a poorer deal without carbon pricing at its core.

Viewpoint 3

> *"Many hope the Green New Deal will help stave off the serious consequences of global warming. Unfortunately, the actual legislation is essentially a progressive policy manifesto—one that will severely damage America's economy."*

The Green New Deal Is a Left-Wing Boondoggle

John Kristof

In the following viewpoint, John Kristof criticizes Congresswoman Alexandria Ocasio-Cortez's 2019 Green New Deal proposal, suggesting that many of its provisions would cause more harm than good. He focuses on three aspects of the proposal: the overall cost of the proposal (which he calculates at $6T annually), the lack of a clear plan to pay for many of its programs, and the inclusion of projects and goals that are not directly related to climate and the environment (e.g., reducing overall income inequality, removing work requirements for welfare, anti-monopoly provisions). Taken as a whole, Kristof argues that the Green New Deal is more an expensive grab-bag of left-wing policy priorities than a sensible plan for environmental reform. John Kristof is a public policy researcher, analyst, and writer who specializes in education and fiscal policy. He is a research fellow at the Sagamore Institute and a research analyst for EdChoice.

"We Can't Afford the Green New Deal," by John Kristof, *The American Conservative*, February 18, 2019. Reprinted by permission.

Can the US Afford to Improve Its Infrastructure with a Green Economy?

As you read, consider the following questions:

1. Which aspects of the Green New Deal does the author identify as overly political and unrelated to environmental goals?
2. What is MMT and why does the author criticize its role in the Green New Deal's original proposal?
3. According to the author, what are some of the downsides of financing the Green New Deal with deficit spending?

She did it. After months of fervor surrounding a potential "Green New Deal" to address the growing problem of climate change, Congresswoman Alexandria Ocasio-Cortez released an official proposal on February 7. The hype surrounding it has already pushed Senate Majority Leader Mitch McConnell to schedule its vote on the Senate floor. Many hope this Green New Deal will help stave off the serious consequences of global warming. Unfortunately, the actual legislation is essentially a progressive policy manifesto—one that will severely damage America's economy.

The opening clauses of the Green New Deal read as you might expect. They cite recent UN and U.S. climate reports on the various consequences countries could face if the average global temperature rises to a certain point. But then the resolution switches gears with comments on "related crises" such as income inequality and wage stagnation. These issues are supposedly connected because climate change disproportionately affects disadvantaged Americans.

The document itself is a whirlwind of ideology. The solutions it offers range from somewhat new goals, such as "reducing risks posed by flooding and other environmental impacts," to impossible projects, like "upgrading all existing buildings in the United States" to be more efficient and sustainable. Most of the climate change-related proposals involve increasing the development of clean tech and infrastructure. But the end of the document devolves into an economic agenda seemingly distinct from the resolution's

America's Infrastructure and the Green Economy

environmental mission, such as a federal jobs guarantee and anti-monopoly provisions.

Even more concerning is the left-wing approach to enforcing this Green New Deal. In a now-deleted "FAQ" posted to Congresswoman Ocasio-Cortez's website, she says that one of her resolution's objectives is to guarantee "economic security to all who are unable or unwilling to work." This hints at removing work requirements for welfare or introducing a universal basic income. Besides income security, Ocasio-Cortez also uses the Green New Deal to theoretically guarantee affordable housing, health care, and higher education to all.

Ocasio-Cortez has since backtracked from the missing FAQ, insisting that an edited version will be released at some future date. But what she deleted revealed a lot about her intentions. If her vision is realized, the Green New Deal will be tremendously expensive. Medicare-for-all alone would require more than $3 trillion per year, nearly doubling current federal spending and potentially lowering health care quality in the U.S. If UBI were to guarantee $10,000 annually to all Americans, federal spending could rise another $3 trillion. Universal college would start by adding nearly a trillion dollars of spending over the next decade, but would likely grow as administrators face even fewer incentives to actually make schools cost-effective. Guaranteeing affordable housing is sure to raise deficits too.

One preliminary analysis calculated the Green New Deal's cost at $6.6 trillion per year, and that's ignoring some of the FAQ's promises. That's equivalent to a third of our GDP, and presuming no other programs are cut, three quarters of the U.S. economy would then be spent by government, the highest rate among developed countries.

This raises Ocasio-Cortez's least favorite question—where is the money for the Green New Deal going to come from?

You might expect her to promote a 70 percent tax on the wealthiest Americans, as she originally suggested back in January. But income and wealth taxes don't show up in the resolution or the online FAQ. Perhaps Ocasio-Cortez decided not to raise the issue after analyses revealed that such a tax on those earning $10 million or more would raise relatively little revenue—just $72 billion a year, enough to keep the federal government open for about one week under current spending levels.

Instead, in her FAQ, Ocasio-Cortez admitted that the Green New Deal would be paid for through borrowing. To defend her position, she posted links to articles promoting Modern Monetary Theory (MMT), a newly popular idea in fiscal policy, which claims that governments can afford whatever they want if they control the currency. Without diving into the details and some of the economic holes, even if a policymaker believed MMT could work in theory, she couldn't claim it would work in the United States. MMT assumes and requires an independent body that sets fiscal policy, like a Federal Reserve, only for budgets rather than monetary decisions. MMT is internally consistent, but that just makes it an accounting trick. Its assumptions are too unrealistic to justify more spending.

And despite the chipper rhetoric behind the Green New Deal, the American people wouldn't actually be better off. Ocasio-Cortez insists we should believe the Green New Deal is an economic possibility because several Western European governments also spend a lot on their economies. But those countries impose high taxes on everyone, not just high-income earners. In fact, the U.S. already has the most progressive tax system of any developed country, five times more progressive than the Scandinavian countries. Make no mistake: a more democratic socialist system would require the vast majority of Americans to pay a lot more in taxes.

Excessive deficit financing should be off the table as well. Such drastic borrowing would be disastrous for the U.S. credit rating, which would require much more money to cover interest payments, pushing aside more desirable investments in welfare assistance, defense, and infrastructure. Those interest payments would mean even more borrowing or inflation to fund the deficit, starting a vicious cycle that could accelerate an economic crisis.

Perhaps Green New Deal supporters are willing to sacrifice the economy if it means saving the planet. But we don't face so dramatic a choice. It is possible to promote green energy and infrastructure without rewriting the entire American economic system. And even if the Green New Deal worked perfectly, a carbon-free America alone will mean little for the trajectory of global climate change. Most of the rising carbon emissions come from China, India, and other countries outside the U.S. and Europe.

Fighting climate change effectively wouldn't be as sexy as the Green New Deal. Some parts of Ocasio-Cortez's proposal should be pursued, such as greater research, development, and the advancement of green energy. Carbon capture technology can mitigate damage until cleaner energy is introduced around more of the globe. Economists love carbon taxes, which could be used to encourage development of those green technologies, and revenues could be rebated back to American households.

Democrats serious about promoting environmental sustainability should follow House Speaker Nancy Pelosi in opposing the Green New Deal. The U.S. economy has grown without consideration for its environmental effects for most of its history, and purporting to stave off a planetary problem without giving up anything is silly. But hard problems require hard work, not out-of-touch ideological manifestos.

VIEWPOINT 4

> "The Green New Deal therefore contains a basic contradiction. [...] Many of the measures proposed—such as investing in infrastructure and spreading wealth more evenly—will intrinsically work in tension with efforts to decarbonise the economy."

The Green New Deal May Boost Carbon Emissions

Matthew Paterson

In the following viewpoint, Matthew Paterson raises questions about the feasibility of the Green New Deal's implied promise—to promote growth and reduce inequality while at the same time decarbonizing the economy and encouraging the development of green technology and infrastructure. He also questions whether a historical example like the New Deal of the 1930s offers an appropriate model for addressing the complex issues associated with climate change and green reform. Matthew Paterson is professor of politics and research director of the Sustainable Consumption Institute at Manchester University. His work focuses on political economy, international governance, and climate policy.

"The Green New Deal's Contradiction—New Infrastructure and Redistribution May Boost Carbon Emissions," by Matthew Paterson, The Conversation, March 6, 2019. https://theconversation.com/the-green-new-deals-contradiction-new-infrastructure-and-redistribution-may-boost-carbon-emissions-112078. Licensed under CC BY-ND-4.0 International.

As you read, consider the following questions:

1. According to the author, how did the original New Deal of the 1930s contribute to "the great acceleration" of high fossil fuel energy use?
2. Why does the author suggest that there is an internal tension between promoting growth and decarbonizing the economy?
3. What are some of the differences between the economic problems facing FDR when he introduced the New Deal and the environmental-economic problems that the Green New Deal proposes to address?

The Green New Deal has broadened imaginations worldwide on the subject of climate change, encouraging people to consider what action to tackle it could do for society. US congresswoman Alexandria Ocasio-Cortez announced the Green New Deal resolution in February 2019, calling for a rapid transition to net zero greenhouse gas emissions, a massive investment in infrastructure and financial redistribution.

While the project would attempt to halt further warming, it would also counter inequality and compensate losers from the energy transition, such as workers in carbon-intensive industries such as coal mining.

It's already helped wrest the political agenda in the US from the regressive policies and scandals of the Trump administration, and has gained bipartisan support among US voters, despite right-wing pundits denouncing it as a communist plot.

The Green New Deal borrows its name and ethos from the New Deal—introduced in the 1930s by then US president Franklin D. Roosevelt to kickstart an economy crippled by the Great Depression. But are strategies that echo the needs of the 1930s and 1940s—ending the Depression and defeating Nazism—suitable for the rapid transition from fossil fuels that defines our needs in the early 21st century?

Can any strategy that relies on historical analogies be adapted to the current climate emergency?

Teaching an Old Deal New Tricks

The Green New Deal's proposed investment in public infrastructure and focus on inequality mirrors the original aims of the New Deal, but economic transformation will look very different under a Green New Deal. Whereas Roosevelt's New Deal aimed to grow the economy, its modern equivalent entails shrinking many economic activities currently central to the economy's operations.

Another way of looking at this is that the original New Deal spurred a massive increase in greenhouse gas emissions. By generating huge public investment in roads and power stations, as well as redistributing wealth through the emerging welfare state, it set the stage for what some call the "great acceleration" in greenhouse gas emissions during and after World War II.

In the US, military build-up was central to this early on, but then it was sustained by the expansion of consumption after the war—most directly by the shift to mass car ownership and urban sprawl that "locked in" high fossil energy use, not only in transport but in housing.

The Green New Deal therefore contains a basic contradiction that anyone pursuing it will have to wrestle with as it develops. Many of the measures proposed—such as investing in infrastructure and spreading wealth more evenly—will intrinsically work in tension with efforts to decarbonise the economy.

They create dynamics that increase energy use at the same time as other parts of the Green New Deal are trying to reduce it. For example, building infrastructure such as new road networks will both create demand for carbon-intensive cement manufacture and opportunities for more people to travel by car.

To reach net zero emissions by sometime early in the second half of the 21st century, as the Paris Agreement and the IPCC Special Report on 1.5°C state we must, the global economy has to decarbonise by at least 3% per year. In rich countries such as the US, this needs to happen more rapidly so that poorer countries, which have contributed less overall to global warming, have more time to adapt.

The targets in the Green New Deal are consistent with this sort of time-frame for decarbonising the global economy. But, even if wealthy countries like the US "only" have to achieve 3% cuts per year, as the economy grows by—say—2%, then in effect the country has to cut emissions by around 5% per year relative to the growing size of the economy. To illustrate the scale of this challenge, historically, emissions have declined relative to GDP by only about 1% per year, in the aftermath of the 2008 recession.

So the challenge is enormous. But of course, the effect of much of the Green New Deal—to invest in infrastructure, to redistribute income—will be to generate significant economic growth. Indeed, this is the point—to get the US economy out of its present stagnation.

But it's hard to see how this will be done without generating new sources of carbon emissions—more housing, more cars and more consumption generally. Herein lies the tension that will recur through the life of the Green New Deal, even if it gets through the immediate quagmire of US politics.

Its supporters will have to manage this tension, even though the vast majority of the US left and environmental movement are behind it.

If one imperative is to build new infrastructure to get the US economy going, how much of this will really do more than pay lip service to the energy system transformation in practice? The "Green" in Green New Deal demands that all new infrastructure built is effectively carbon neutral.

Even new transit infrastructure, for example, would have to be entirely electric, at the same time as that electricity system is supposed to rapidly abandon coal and then natural gas. It's easy to imagine which will win when that tension works its way through the political process.

It's not that the Green New Deal isn't worth pursuing—it's an extremely promising development. It's just important to remember Naomi Klein's invocation that "this changes everything"—dealing with climate change is unlikely to lend itself to off-the-shelf solutions from an earlier age.

Viewpoint 5

> "The unseriousness of the Green New Deal stems not just from its economic illiteracy but also because of its environmental illiteracy."

There Are Various Problems with the Green New Deal

Steven F. Hayward

In the following viewpoint, Steven F. Hayward introduces five separate but related problems with the Green New Deal, as rendered in Congresswoman Alexandria Ocasio-Cortez's 2019 proposal. He begins by suggesting that the program's model—the New Deal of the 1930s—was not as successful as Americans believe, and that this modern version suffers from some of the same basic problems as the original plan. He focuses particularly on the proposal's opposition to nuclear power, which he argues could offer tremendous benefits and help the United States meet its power needs while reducing the deleterious environmental effects of economic activity. Steven F. Hayward is currently a resident scholar at the Institute of Governmental Studies at UC Berkeley and visiting lecturer at Berkeley's Boalt Hall Law School.

"Five Reasons the Green New Deal Is Worse Than You Thought," by Steven F. Hayward, The Bulwark, February 12, 2019. Reprinted by permission.

Can the US Afford to Improve Its Infrastructure with a Green Economy?

As you read, consider the following questions:

1. Why does the author believe that the authors of the Green New Deal should re-think their position on nuclear power?
2. According to the author, what are some of the benefits of our current economy's high reliance on fossil fuel–based energy?
3. What are some of the environmental policy measures the author identifies as having been excluded from the Green New Deal proposal?

It is hard to say whether the "Green New Deal" announced last week is the Democratic Party's suicide note for the 2020 election cycle, or an epic troll that will trap Republicans into a climate policy "compromise" that they don't really want and won't really work. Let's look it over from five different angles.

(1) It's tempting to dismiss the Green New Deal by suggesting that it would probably work no better than the original New Deal. (The conventional wisdom is that the New Deal ended the Great Depression, but some revisionist economic historians suggest that it probably prolonged it.) But that misses the point that the New Deal remains an iconic, almost magical, symbol in American politics. Most Americans still have the impression that the New Deal was one of the great initiatives in American history, and aren't much impressed with revisionist econometric analysis about its mediocre (and often negative) economic effects. Score one for good labeling.

(2) The unseriousness of the Green New Deal stems not just from its economic illiteracy but also because of its environmental illiteracy. Never mind Alexandria Ocasio-Cortez's spectacular belly-flops about eliminating cow farts and airplanes: To achieve its stated goal of eliminating the use of fossil fuels in a decade (or by any future date) will require electrifying everything, including all home heating and transportation that are currently supplied by fossil fuels.

This would require probably tripling our electricity production, assuming that we can even get practical electric-powered cars, trucks, and trains at scale (never mind electric airplanes). This simply isn't possible with wind and solar power.

And even if you could generate the power that way (and again: you can't) battery storage is another tremendous challenge. Get back to me when you've worked out the materials requirements for an at least thousand-fold increase in the mining, production, and disposal of lithium-ion batteries or their successors.

And even if you could get the raw materials of lithium, cobalt, copper, platinum, and other metals necessary for the windmills, solar panels, and batteries you would need, the environmental impact of this supply-chain—not to mention its carbon footprint—could be larger than the impact of oil, gas, and coal production today.

And then, just for fun, consider the requirements in the raw materials—and skilled workforce—that would be necessary for retrofitting every building in America, as AOC's talking points propose.

Very few environmentalists ever factor these costs into their fantasy calculations of a fossil-free future. And AOC isn't one of them.

(3) AOC's Green New Deal wants to reduce carbon emissions while phasing out the largest source of non-carbon energy we currently have—nuclear power. The level of whimsy here is matched only by the aspects of the plan that add universal healthcare, a job guarantee, and ending racism as essential parts of its environmentalist vision.

Why not add world peace and education reform while we're at it?

The narrowness of the anti-nuclear attitude of the Green New Deal appears to be either willful or ignorant. One of the quiet revolutions taking place inside much of the environmental movement today is a reckoning with its opposition to nuclear power a generation ago. Many prominent environmentalists such as James Hansen now argue that nuclear power is essential for reducing greenhouse gas emissions. It is no coincidence that the advanced nations with the lowest greenhouse gas emission rates are those with high amounts of nuclear energy, such as France and Sweden. (Kudos to those environmentalists who have publicly broken with the rigid orthodoxy of the past.)

There are, however, two ways in which it is possible to take the Green New Deal a little more seriously, though in ways that could backfire for it.

First, if you believe in the catastrophic climate change scenario if we don't cap atmospheric carbon dioxide concentrations below 450 parts per million (we're currently a little above 400 ppm, but the level is growing about 1.5 ppm per year), climate policy orthodoxy says we need to do exactly what the Green New Deal proposes—the virtual elimination of all fossil fuels on a very short timeline. And if you take this scenario seriously, it would mean elimination of fossil fuels is necessary for the entire world—not just the United States.

How would that work?

Never mind that the Green New Deal proposes no specific and measurable technologies to achieve this global goal. The point is that none of the previous climate policy initiatives, whether the Kyoto Protocol of 1998, the Paris Climate Accord of 2015, or President Obama's Clean Power Plan came anywhere close to this emission reduction target. This is one reason James Hansen departs from the façade of most environmentalists in declaring the Paris Climate Accord to be a "fraud." The Green New Deal, by setting out ending fossil fuel use as its explicit goal, is calling the bluff of the current pantomime policy.

(There's also the economic fact that if the United States were to eliminate its reliance on fossil fuels, this would drive the price of oil down, thereby allowing developing countries to use more of it in their drive to modernize.)

(4) In addition to the economically ruinous cost of attempting the Green New Deal, it might force a consideration of the environmental calculus that is deliberately avoided today: Are the tradeoffs from our civilization's use of fossil fuels overwhelmingly

positive, even with the potential damages from climate change in the future? The answer is at least a qualified "yes." But currently, this is not something you are allowed to say in polite society.

However, the massive dislocations (not to mention exorbitant costs) of the Green New Deal may give people room to say, publicly, "thanks, but no thanks." It's one thing to be for "the environment" when the cost is a carbon tax. It's another thing entirely when you're talking about a wholesale reorganization of society and the economy.

And the more people take the Green New Deal seriously, the more favorable our current fossil fuel regime will look. As will cheaper (and probably more effective) measures such as more nuclear power, carbon-capture technologies, and solar-radiation management—three serious options deliberately excluded from the Green New Deal because they conflict with the fundamentalist orthodoxy of the climate change fanatics.

(5) But there is still a hazard for Republicans. It is fine to hoot about the extravagance of the Green New Deal, but given that it is not acceptable in polite society to contest the doomsday scenario of climate change (this is a subject for another day), the Green New Dealers will be able to say, "Fine—what have you got? We've at least proposed something of grand ambition that meets the 'crisis.'"

A number of Republicans in the House and Senate have been stumbling around for a while looking for a way to weigh in sensibly on climate change policy, and it is not hard to imagine the crafty Speaker Pelosi offering a "compromise" on some climate measures—a carbon tax or some far-reaching energy performance standards perhaps—that would be the thin end of a large wedge of climate policy takeover of the nation's energy sector. This is right out of the Trump playbook: Ask for something outrageous, and get some of what you really want.

In other words, like the original New Deal, the Green New Deal might not work as advertised, but it might work for Democrats.

Periodical and Internet Sources Bibliography

The following articles have been selected to supplement the diverse views presented in this chapter.

Heather Clancy, "How Infrastructure Is Banking on Green Banks," GreenBiz.com, March 25, 2021, https://www.greenbiz.com/article/how-infrastructure-banking-green-banks.

Tyler Cowen, "The Best Way to Judge Any Green Energy Policy," Bloomberg Opinion, June 17, 2021, https://www.bloomberg.com/opinion/articles/2021-06-17/green-energy-the-issue-is-politics-not-technology-or-cost.

Molly Lempriere, "Green Workforce of the Future Being 'Undermined' by Lack of Government Policy," Current News, October 25, 2021, https://www.current-news.co.uk/news/green-workforce-of-the-future-being-undermined-by-lack-of-government-policy.

Jonathan Neale, "Jobs Not COPs," *The Ecologist*, November 2, 2021, https://theecologist.org/2021/nov/02/jobs-not-cops.

Ben Ritz, "How to Strengthen the Bipartisan Infrastructure Framework by Controlling Costs," The Hill, July 12, 2021, https://thehill.com/opinion/finance/562506-how-to-strengthen-the-bipartisan-infrastructure-framework-by-controlling.

Christian Sagers, "Is a $2.3 Trillion Infrastructure Plan Right for America?" *Deseret News*, April 14, 2021, https://www.deseret.com/opinion/2021/4/14/22380121/joe-biden-2-3-trillion-infrastructure-plan-right-for-america-national-debt.

Alex Seitz-Wald, "Climate vs. Jobs: How Democrats Talk About Policy Proposals May Make the Difference," NBC News, October 25, 2021, https://www.nbcnews.com/politics/congress/climate-vs-jobs-how-democrats-talk-about-policy-proposals-may-n1282238.

Adie Tomer, Caroline George, and Joseph W. Kane, "Rethinking Climate Finance to Improve Infrastructure Resilience," Brookings Institution, June 22, 2021, https://www.brookings.edu/research/rethinking-climate-finance-to-improve-infrastructure-resilience.

Gernot Wagner, "Why Biden's Infrastructure Plan Is a Green Jobs Plan," Bloomberg Green, April 2, 2021, https://www.bloomberg.com/news/articles/2021-04-02/why-biden-s-infrastructure-plan-is-a-green-jobs-plan.

OPPOSING VIEWPOINTS® SERIES

CHAPTER 3

Can a Green Economy Drive the Economic Growth That America Needs?

Chapter Preface

For much of the twentieth century, economic growth in the United States was driven by a liberal regulatory environment, the availability of cheap fuel and materials, and aggressive consumer appetites. In one way or another, the green reform movement seeks to mitigate each of these conditions, and economists and business experts have questioned whether a green economy can sustain similar levels of growth and prosperity.

Advocates for climate and environmental reform have responded to these concerns by highlighting the growth of clean energy and other green industries in recent years. The economists Christina DiPasquale and Kate Gordon offer the following:

> The clean energy sector is growing at a rate of 8.3 percent. Solar thermal energy expanded by 18.4 percent annually from 2003 to 2010, along with solar photovoltaic power by 10.7 percent, and biofuels by 8.9 percent over the same period. Meanwhile, the U.S. wind energy industry saw 35 percent average annual growth over the past five years, accounting for 35 percent of new U.S. power capacity in that period, according to the 2010 U.S. Wind Industry Annual Market Report. As a whole, the clean energy sector's average growth rate of 8.3 percent annually during this period was nearly double the growth rate of the overall economy during that time.[1]

These numbers may be compelling, but the debate on green reform extends well beyond clean energy solutions.

For instance, it may be true that appliances are more energy efficient that those of previous generations, but today's consumers typically own and use many more appliances than in the past. The latter trend has supported economic growth but has also created a rebound effect and limited the impact of efficiency enhancements. Activists associated with the degrowth movement have suggested that a truly green economy may require that consumers tame their appetite for new products. But consumer spending accounts for

70 percent of the US economy, and it's difficult to imagine how a steep drop in consumer demand could occur without significant disruptive effects in the economy as a whole. The viewpoints in this chapter cover several different perspectives on the conditions that impact economic growth in the United States and how various green reform efforts might affect those conditions.

Notes

1. "Top 10 Reasons Why Green Jobs Are Vital to Our Economy," by Christina DiPasquale and Kate Gordon, Center for American Progress, September 7, 2011.

Viewpoint 1

> "If we succeed, through the Green New Deal, in increasing the efficiency at which these industries consume energy and we also deliver abundant supplies of clean renewable energy, then the problems of dealing with energy-intensive industries can be solved."

Degrowth Policies Cannot Avert Climate Crisis

C. J. Polychroniou

In the following viewpoint, C. J. Polychroniou interviews Robert Pollin, a professor of economics and director of the Political Economy Research Institute (PERI) at the University of Massachusetts Amherst. Their discussion focuses on the differences between reform- and innovation-based policy proposals like the Green New Deal and the more radical ideas associated with the degrowth movement. Pollin is highly critical of the degrowth movement, which he views as underdeveloped and lacking in the specificity and detail necessary for real policy action. Instead of embracing a vague and idealistic vision like degrowth, Pollin argues, we should focus on reform and innovation, and double down on the more concrete measures included in the Green New Deal proposal. C. J. Polychroniou is a columnist for Global Policy, a contributing writer for Truthout, and a policy fellow at the Levy Economics Institute at Bard College.

"Degrowth Policies Cannot Avert Climate Crisis. We Need a Green New Deal," by C. J. Polychroniou, © Truthout.org, July 3, 2021. Reprinted by permission.

As you read, consider the following questions:

1. What are some of the main problems with the degrowth movement and its literature, according to Pollin?
2. What does "decoupling" refer to in the context of climate policy and green reform?
3. Why does Pollin believe that innovation is a better strategy than degrowth when it comes to addressing the impact of resource-intensive industries like steel, concrete, and transportation?

The Green New Deal is the boldest and most likely the most effective way to combat the climate emergency. According to its advocates, the Green New Deal will save the planet while boosting economic growth and generating in the process millions of new and well-paying jobs. However, a growing number of ecological economists contend that rescuing the environment necessitates "degrowth."

To the extent that a sharp reduction in economic activity is a positive goal, "degrowth" requires overturning the current world order. But do we have the luxury to wait for a new world order while the catastrophic impacts of global warming are already upon us and getting worse with each passing decade?

World-renowned progressive economist Robert Pollin, distinguished professor of economics and co-director of the Political Economy Research Institute at the University of Massachusetts-Amherst, is one of the leading proponents of a global Green New Deal. In this interview, he addresses the degrowth vs. Green New Deal debate, looking at how economies can grow while still advancing a viable climate stabilization project as long as the growth process is absolutely decoupled from fossil fuel consumption.

C.J. Polychroniou: Since the idea of a Green New Deal entered into public consciousness, the debate about climate emergency is becoming increasingly polarized between those

advocating "green growth" and those arguing in support of "degrowth." What exactly does "degrowth" mean, and is this at the end of the day an economic or an ideological debate?

Robert Pollin: Let me first say that I don't think that the debate on the climate emergency between advocates of degrowth versus the Green New Deal is becoming increasingly polarized, certainly not as a broad generalization. Rather, as an advocate of the Green New Deal and critic of degrowth, I would still say that there are large areas of agreement along with some significant differences. For example, I agree that uncontrolled economic growth produces serious environmental damage along with increases in the supply of goods and services that households, businesses and governments consume. I also agree that a significant share of what is produced and consumed in the current global capitalist economy is wasteful, especially much, if not most, of what high-income people throughout the world consume. It is also obvious that growth per se as an economic category makes no reference to the distribution of the costs and benefits of an expanding economy. I think it is good to keep in mind both the areas of agreement as well as the differences.

But what about definitions: What do we actually mean by the Green New Deal and degrowth?

Starting with the Green New Deal: The Intergovernmental Panel on Climate Change (IPCC) estimates that for the global economy to move onto a viable climate stabilization path, global emissions of carbon dioxide (CO_2) will have to fall by about 45 percent as of 2030 and reach net zero emissions by 2050. As such, by my definition, the core of the global Green New Deal is to advance a global project to hit these IPCC targets, and to accomplish this in a way that also expands decent job opportunities and raises mass living standards for working people and the poor throughout the world. The single most important project within the Green New Deal entails phasing out the consumption of oil, coal and natural gas to produce energy, since burning fossil fuels is responsible for about 70-75 percent of all global CO_2 emissions.

We then have to build an entirely new global energy infrastructure, the centerpieces of which are high efficiency and clean renewable energy sources—primarily solar and wind power. The investments required to dramatically increase energy efficiency standards and to equally dramatically expand the global supply of clean energy sources will also be a huge source of new job creation, in all regions of the world. These are the basics of the Green New Deal as I see it. It is that simple in concept, while also providing specific pathways for achieving its overarching goals.

Now on degrowth: Since I am not a supporter, it would be unfair for me to be the one explaining what it means. So here is how some of the leading degrowth proponents themselves describe the concept and movement. For example, in a 2015 edited volume titled *Degrowth: A Vocabulary for a New Era*, the volume's editors Giacomo D'Alisa, Federico Demaria and Giorgos Kallis write that, "The foundational theses of degrowth are that growth is uneconomic and unjust, that it is ecologically unsustainable and that it will never be enough." More recently, a 2021 paper by Riccardo Mastini, Giorgos Kallis and Jason Hickel, titled "A Green New Deal Without Growth?," write that "ecological economists have defined degrowth as an equitable downscaling of throughput, with a concomitant securing of wellbeing."

It is instructive here that, in this 2021 paper, Mastini, Kallis and Hickel do also acknowledge that degrowth has not advanced into developing a specific set of economic programs, writing that "degrowth is not a political platform, but rather an 'umbrella concept' that brings together a wide variety of ideas and social struggles." This acknowledgement reflects, in my view, a major ongoing weakness with the degrowth literature, which is that, in concerning itself primarily with very broad themes, it actually gives almost no detailed attention to developing an effective climate stabilization project, or any other specific ecological project. Indeed, this deficiency was reflected in a 2017 interview with the leading ecological economist Herman Daly himself, without question a major intellectual progenitor of the degrowth movement. Daly says in the interview that he is "favorably inclined" toward degrowth, but nevertheless demurs that he is "still waiting for them to get beyond the slogan and develop something a little more concrete."

This lack of specificity among degrowth proponents leads to further problems. For example, degrowth supporters, such as Mastini et al. in their 2021 paper, are clear that they support the transformation of the global energy system along the lines that I have described above, from our current fossil fuel-dominant system to one whose core features are high efficiency and clean renewable energy sources. Yet in fact, building out this new energy system will obviously entail massive growth of the global clean energy system, just as it will equally entail the phasing out—or degrowth, if you prefer—of the global fossil fuel energy system. In my view, it is more useful to be specific about which sectors of the global economy will certainly need to grow—e.g., the clean energy system—while others, like fossil fuels, contract, as opposed to invoking sweeping generalities about degrowth. We can extend this point. For example, I am sure degrowth proponents would favor major expansions in access to public education, universal health care, high-quality affordable housing, regenerative agriculture and the share of the Earth's surface covered by forests.

In focusing on some critical specifics, I would also add that there is no way that a general project of degrowth can put the global economy onto a viable climate stabilization path. With the COVID-19 recession, the global economy just went through a powerful natural experiment to demonstrate this point. That is, during the pandemic in 2020, the global economy contracted by 3.5 percent, which the International Monetary Fund described as a "severe collapse … that has had acute adverse impacts on women, youth, the poor, the informally employed and those who work in contact-intensive sectors." In other words, the pandemic produced an intense period of global "degrowth." This recession did also produce a decline in emissions, as entire sections of the global economy were forced into lockdown mode. But the emissions decline amounted to only 6.4 percent over 2020. Remember, the

IPCC tells us that we need to cut emissions by 45 percent as of 2030 and be at zero emissions by 2050. If the COVID recession only yields a 6.4 percent emissions reduction despite the enormous levels of economic pain inflicted, clearly "degrowth" cannot come close, on its own, to delivering a 45-percent emissions cut by 2030, much less a zero emissions global economy by 2050.

Those who see the Green New Deal not only as the most effective strategy to tackle global warming but also as an engine for growth, such as yourself, rely on the concept of "decoupling," by which is meant the absolute decoupling of economic growth from carbon emissions. However, degrowth advocates seem to be arguing that there is no empirical evidence for absolute "decoupling," and that it's highly unlikely that it will ever happen. How do you respond to such claims?

Let's recognize, to begin with, that people are still going to need to consume energy to light, heat and cool buildings; to power cars, buses, trains and airplanes; and to operate computers and industrial machinery, among other uses. As one critical example here, in low-income economies, delivering adequate supplies of affordable electricity becomes transformative for people's lives, enabling them, for example, to adequately light their homes at night rather than relying on kerosene lanterns. As such, it should be our goal to greatly expand access to electricity to low-income communities throughout the world, while we are also driving down CO_2 emissions to zero. The solution is for energy consumption and economic activity more generally to be absolutely decoupled from the generation of CO_2 emissions. That is, the consumption of fossil fuel energy will need to fall steadily and dramatically in absolute terms, even while people will still be able to consume energy resources to meet their various demands. The more modest goal of relative decoupling—through which fossil fuel energy consumption and CO_2 emissions continue to increase, but at a slower rate than overall economic activity—is therefore not a solution. Economies can still continue to grow while still advancing a viable climate stabilization project as long as the growth process is absolutely decoupled from fossil fuel consumption.

Is absolute decoupling impossible to accomplish within the context of economic growth? To date, we have seen some modest evidence—and I do stress the evidence is modest—of absolute decoupling taking place. For example, between 2000 and 2014, 21 countries, including the U.S., Germany, the U.K., Spain and Sweden, all managed to absolutely decouple GDP growth from CO_2 emissions—i.e., GDP in these countries expanded over this 14-year period while CO_2 emissions fell. This is a positive development, but only a small step in the right direction.

The way to deliver a much more rapid pattern of absolute decoupling is, of course, to build out the global clean energy economy, and to do so quickly. This is a feasible project. By my own estimates, it requires that the global economy spend approximately 2.5 percent of global GDP per year on investments in energy efficiency and clean renewable energy supplies, while the global economy grows at an average rate of about 3 percent per year between now and 2050. The International Renewable Energy Agency and International Energy Agency recently published studies that reached similar results for the global economy. Focused on the U.S. economy, the energy economists Jim Williams and Ryan Jones also reached a similar result, as part of the Zero Carbon Action Plan project.

From this and related evidence, I conclude that absolute decoupling is certainly a feasible, though also obviously a hugely challenging, project. But we can't just talk about it, pro or con. We have to make the investments, at 2.5 percent of global GDP per year or thereabouts, every year until 2050, to build the global clean energy economy. If we do that, absolute decoupling will happen. If we don't make those investments, then of course, absolute decoupling becomes an impossibility.

Various ecologically minded activists are also arguing that the Green New Deal relies on the use of massive energy resources,

including extensive use of the steel industry, in order to make the transition to a clean, renewable and net-zero emissions economy, and that what is really needed instead is a green revolution of the mind, whereby zero energy living is the ultimate goal. My question is this: Can the Green New Deal deliver 100 percent clean energy?

There are several industries in which energy is consumed intensively. They include steel, cement and paper, along with, obviously, all forms of transportation. But note that these industries are energy intensive. They are not necessarily fossil fuel energy intensive. If we succeed, through the Green New Deal, in increasing the efficiency at which these industries consume energy and we also deliver abundant supplies of clean renewable energy, then the problems of dealing with energy-intensive industries can be solved. It's true that there will be some specific areas that will present more difficult challenges. For example, some parts of steel production rely on furnaces that are operating at very high temperatures. Reaching these high temperatures are, to date, difficult to achieve through electricity as opposed to burning coal in a furnace. This problem will need to be solved over time. One likely solution could be to rely on laser technology through which the required high temperatures can be reached with electricity, with the electricity, in turn, being produced through renewable energy.

Another more difficult area is long-distance aviation. To date, we cannot rely on electric batteries to fly planes across the Atlantic Ocean, for example, as we can to drive cars from New York to California. One likely solution here will be to fuel the planes' engines with low-emissions liquid bioenergy, such as ethanol produced from agricultural wastes as the raw material. Battery storage capacities are also likely to be improving significantly with more people focusing on solving exactly this problem. Let's remember that the costs of producing electricity from solar photovoltaic panels have fallen by over 80 percent within the past nine years, and the U.S. Energy Department itself projects further major declines in just the next five years. Moreover, the

International Renewable Agency reported just recently that, for the first time, 62 percent of all renewable energy sources produced energy at lower costs than the cheapest sources of fossil fuel energy.

All of this tells me that achieving absolute decoupling is a feasible project within the framework of a global Green New Deal. The Green New Deal, in turn, is, in my view, the only way through which climate stabilization can become fully consistent with expanding decent work opportunities, raising mass living standards and fighting poverty in all regions of the world.

VIEWPOINT 2

> "In the US, nearly ten times more people were employed in the green economy and its supply chains than employed directly in the fossil fuel industry."

Green Economic Growth Is Real and Thriving

Lucien Georgeson and Mark Maslin

In the following viewpoint, Lucien Georgeson and Mark Maslin introduce their original research on revenue and employment growth in the global green economy, which indicates that the green economy is growing considerably faster and adding more jobs than the fossil fuel industry, particularly in the United States. They also examine the impact of domestic politics on green economic growth, arguing that reform plans like the Green New Deal are more likely to encourage overall economic growth than President Trump's fossil fuel–friendly policies. Lucien Georgeson is a senior analyst at Trove Research and a policy adviser for the Rockefeller Foundation's Economic Council on Planetary Health. Mark Maslin is a professor of Earth system science at University College London.

"US Green Economy's Growth Dwarfs the Fossil Fuel Industry's," by Lucien Georgeson and Mark Maslin, The Conversation, October 15, 2019. https://theconversation.com/us-green-economy-growth-dwarfs-donald-trumps-highest-hopes-for-the-fossil-fuel-industry-123062. Licensed under CC BY-ND-4.0 International.

Can a Green Economy Drive the Economic Growth That America Needs?

As you read, consider the following questions:

1. How did President Trump's rhetoric and policies affect the United States' competitive position in the global green economy?
2. What is the current growth rate of the green economy in America? How does it compare to the growth rate of the fossil fuel industry?
3. How do fossil fuel subsidies affect the United States' ability to innovate and compete in the global green economy?

While US President Donald Trump may be "the world's most powerful climate change denier," our latest research suggests that he took over a thriving green economy.

According to new data, by 2016 it was generating more than US$1.3 trillion in annual revenue and employed approximately 9.5m people—making it the largest green market in the world. It's been growing rapidly too—between 2013 and 2016, both the industry's value and employment figures grew by 20%.

For some time, economic data on the green economy in many countries has been lacking. In the US, the Bureau of Labor Statistics stopped measuring jobs in the green economy in March 2013 due to budget cuts. This meant that US politicians were not able to make informed decisions about the relative merits of supporting green industry or backing fossil fuels—as Trump had pledged to do on his 2016 campaign trail.

To fill this knowledge gap, we analysed massive databases to record the latest available business transactions from every country in the world. We estimated sales revenue and employment figures across 24 economic sub-sectors covering renewable energy, environmental protection, and low carbon goods and services—collectively termed the green economy. We used this same standardised method across all countries, allowing us to make meaningful comparisons between them.

Our study estimates that revenue in the global green economy was $7.87 trillion in 2016. At $1.3 trillion, the US made up 16.5% of the global market—the largest in the world.

Our analysis also suggests that in the US, nearly ten times more people were employed in the green economy and its supply chains (9.5m) than employed directly in the fossil fuel industry (roughly 1m)—that is, miners, electricity grid workers, infrastructure manufacturers and construction workers. This wide gap comes despite the US fossil fuel industry receiving huge subsidies, estimated at $649 billion in 2015 alone.

America First?

Importantly, the green economy has been growing faster than Trump's wildest dreams for the fossil fuel industry. As a presidential candidate in 2016, Trump set out his "America first" energy policy, promising to add 400,000 new jobs to the fossil fuel industry. During the campaign, he suggested that he could increase the industry's economic output by $700bn over 30 years.

Our data indicates that the green economy grew by over $60bn per year 2013 and 2016. This dwarfs Trump's best hopes for growth in the fossil fuel industry, which equate to an annual increase in value of $23bn.

Employment in the US green economy also grew by the equivalent of 1.5m full-time jobs during this time, whereas coal mining jobs declined by 37,000 over the same period.

A Precarious Position

These are strong numbers. But after three years of faltering support, the US's position as a world leader in the green economy is precarious.

Up to now, Trump's campaign rhetoric has not been backed up by major policy changes, although his rollback of a number of

Obama era regulations has likely helped the fossil fuel industry in the short term. But unlike Trump, competing superpowers are strongly backing renewables.

China, for example, has emerged as a global climate leader in the wake of Trump's determination to pull out of the Paris Agreement. In 2017, it announced plans to invest USD$361 billion in clean energy by 2020 to generate 13 million jobs. This investment alone could go a long way to closing the gap between the value of the US's green economy and that of China's, the second largest in the world. Other countries are also poised to overtake the US in the race to shape the global green economy.

The Green New Deal—popularised by Congresswoman Alexandria Ocasio-Cortez and others—is an ambitious policy agenda that could reestablish the US's commitment to the green economy. It proposes massive investment in renewable energy and an environment-friendly public works programme of gargantuan scale. Phasing out direct fossil fuel subsides could free up some of the funding required for such investment.

It's not for us to say whether the Green New Deal is right for the US. But what our data does say loud and clear is this: if you want a strong economy that supports thousands of new jobs, then supporting its green quarters is essential. And of course, it will help our imperiled living planet too.

VIEWPOINT 3

> "Green growth is a project with a utopian charge, depicting a path to the future that claims to be capable of redressing the accumulated harms of the 'old' industrial paradigm."

Green Growth Is a More Tenuous Proposition Than Advocates Suggest

Manu V. Mathai, Jose A. Puppim de Oliveira, and Gareth Dale

In the following excerpted viewpoint, Manu V. Mathai, Jose A. Puppim de Oliveira, and Gareth Dale criticize the green growth paradigm that dominates much of the modern environmental reform movement. Their argument focuses on two key areas: (1) the challenges associated with implementing the green growth model in still-developing economies; and (2) the green growth model's failure to challenge the modern capitalist notion that economic growth is inherently positive. They suggest that we may need to engage in a broader discussion about the nature of modern society and its economic distribution systems in order to address the deep roots of contemporary environmental problems. Manu V. Mathai is assistant professor in the School of Development at Azim Premji University. Jose A. Puppim de Oliveira is a research affiliate at MIT. Gareth Dale is a lecturer in politics at the University of Wales, Swansea, and a senior lecturer in political economy at Brunel University London.

"The Rise and Flaws of Green Growth," by Manu V. Mathai, Jose A. Puppim de Oliveira, and Gareth Dale, *APN Science Bulletin*, May 11, 2018. doi (10.30852/sb.2018.359). Reprinted by permission.

Can a Green Economy Drive the Economic Growth That America Needs?

As you read, consider the following questions:

1. What do the authors mean when they refer to the "progressive state" of modern capitalism?
2. What are some of the disadvantages of the growth-oriented philosophy that the authors identify as a core value of modern capitalist society?
3. Why do developing economies pose a unique challenge for global efforts to reduce carbon emissions?

[…]

"Green growth," together with the related "green economy," represents the latest phase in the reconstruction of political discourse in the face of ecological challenges and environmental movements. It encompasses approaches ranging from geo-engineering mega-projects to routine "efficiency strategies." By such means, green growth promises to stem the environmental crisis and mitigate its consequences whilst simultaneously addressing social challenges of destitution and disempowerment by accelerating economic growth. Green growth is a project with a utopian charge, depicting a path to the future that, thanks to scientific insight, engineering sophistication and managerial smartness, claims to be capable of redressing the accumulated harms of the "old" industrial paradigm. At the same time, at least in its mainstream variants, it claims to embody a sober realism: the route towards a sustainable future maintains, and even reinforces, the institutional and normative territory of the current political economic prevalent ideas.

Taken at face value, green growth appears impervious to critique. Economic growth is taken as good, imperative, essentially limitless, and a matter of pressing concern for society as a whole. And green growth owes much of its influence given that it charts a pathway for continued economic growth even in the face of the environmental crisis and criticisms thereof. Further, the project of economic growth is not easily dislodged. It flows from fundamental societal transformations associated with the advent of modernity (the linearization of time, the notion of progress, the dissolution of just wage norms, and the quantification of processes of wealth, production and distribution). Institutionally, the growth imperative is an inherent attribute of the capitalist mode of production exacerbated under the neoclassical economics paradigm. This capitalism "distinguishes itself from all other socio-economic systems in human history by the movement towards the infinite"; its totalising logic penetrates society in all its facets and converts "almost the entire world into a field of valorisation" (Mahnkopf, 2016) through "the process of competitive, blind accumulation that grants to capitalism its distinctive requirement for relentless growth" (Meadway, 2016).

In an early effort to characterize and justify the economic growth paradigm, Adam Smith speculated that it is "in the progressive state," when society "is advancing to the further acquisition, rather than when it has acquired its full complement of riches that the condition of the labouring poor, of the great body of the people, seems to be the happiest" (Smith, 1776, p. 81). It is in a state of continual economic growth that emancipatory potential is achieved, and not just wealth. And, indeed, the subsequent two centuries of industrial capitalism did significantly advance the "acquisition of riches," as well as raise life expectancy, erode feudal and patrimonial forms of personal economic dependence, and catalyse advances in individual liberty and democracy that, although geographically very uneven in quality and application, were global in scale and momentous in scope.

This narrative of the "progressive state" of capitalist modernity is now struggling to retain its coherence in three respects. One is internal to the growth paradigm itself. The system's own yardstick of success, GDP per capita growth (annual %), has for several decades followed a flat and even downward trajectory in many countries (World Bank, 2017). Although global capitalism is systemically "compelled towards growth," it appears to be "decreasingly able to deliver it" (Meadway, 2016). The second is a scepticism vis-

Can a Green Economy Drive the Economic Growth That America Needs?

The Green New Deal Would Be Detrimental to the U.S. Economy

There are a multitude of problems with the Green New Deal, including unattainable goals that will leave the American economy in shambles and crush the working class, all while not even solving the original problem.

The main problem with most "green energy" legislation is the unrealistic goals. A majority of the goals within these resolutions don't account for the enormous strain the economy would be put under. In the Green New Deal, Rep. Alexandria Ocasio-Cortez and Sen. Ed Markey want to try "upgrading all existing buildings in the United States" and "building or upgrading to energy-efficient, distributed, and 'smart' power grids." This would plunge the American economy into shambles. By attempting to upgrade all existing buildings and power grids, the U.S. government would need to generate trillions of dollars. The only way they could hope to attain that much money would be to tax the American people into oblivion.

The Green New Deal hopes to "provide unprecedented levels of prosperity and economic security for all people of the United States" but will only widen the socio-economic chasm. The Green New Deal hopes to phase out the coal and fossil fuel industries entirely. Approximately 1,122,700 jobs are created by the fossil fuel industry and a majority of them are held by blue-collar workers. Among the hardest hit will be our American farmers. Farmers rely on fossil fuels from combines and tractors to fertilizers and pesticides and taking away gasoline and diesel will render family farms inoperable. The rich and powerful, like Ocasio-Cortez, advocate for the destruction of millions of Americans' livelihoods all while traveling on private jets that guzzle thousands of gallons of gas.

The largest problem with the Green New Deal is it doesn't account for the Chinese Communist Party. The Green New Deal wants America to reduce greenhouse gas emissions to net-zero by 2030 but fails to mention that China accounts for 30% of the global greenhouse gases emitted and they continually increase emissions each year.

"The Green New Deal Would Be Detrimental to the U.S. Economy," by Alex Whipple, *Mill Valley News*, April 14, 2021.

à-vis the "Smithian promise" that growth will emancipate the poor. Against a backdrop of vulgar levels of income inequality, the supposed connection between economic growth and social wellbeing has been increasingly called into question by prominent studies (Stiglitz, Sen & Fitoussi, 2009). Some critics argue that "just when the human species discovers that the environment cannot absorb further increases in emissions, we also learn that further economic growth in the developed world no longer improves health, happiness or wellbeing" (Pickett & Wilkinson, 2009; p.215).

The third is a growth scepticism fuelled by concerns over the diminishing ecological space available to supply non-renewable resources and to absorb the effluents of ongoing growth. Ecological thresholds are being breached, and "tipping points" appear to be upon us (Rockstrom et al., 2009). To this, the dominant response has long been one or another variant of "green growth": the idea that investment in the production of knowledge and science, the resulting innovations in technique, environmental awareness that purportedly comes with rising incomes, and a structural shift toward less resource- and energy-intensive service sector industries will "save the planet" (Tierney, 2009). In its formalized version, this idea came to be known as the Environmental Kuznets Curve (EKC). The EKC holds that, after a certain point, economic growth correlates strongly with greater efficiency in resource use. However, the idea that a simple, inverse relationship exists between per capita income and environmental stress has been challenged on a number of counts. For example, the idea that caring about the environment is a privilege of rich people is baseless; it ignores the "environmentalism of the poor" (Down to Earth, 1993, Martinez-Alier et al., 2016 and Kothari, 2016). Moreover, the EKC hypothesis has held in particular conditions, with respect for example to pollutants that have short-term costs, such as particulates, and not with respect to accumulating wastes or to pollutants involving long-term costs, such as greenhouse gas emissions (GHGs). The EKC hypothesis ignores the fact that reduced pollution in developed countries is often part of the same processes—above all, the outsourcing of manufacturing, and consequently pollution, to developing countries—that determine the expansion of resource-intensive production elsewhere (Sunderlin, 2003, p. 161).

A major hope of green growth advocates, on which much of their case rests, is that efficiency gains will negate overall increments in attendant energy and material throughput, including a dramatic reduction of GHG emissions. But this is much too sanguine, not least because it neglects to consider the "Jevons Paradox," which postulates that the improved technological efficiency in the utilization of a natural resource, within a capitalist framework, tends not to decrease but to increase its overall rate of consumption, because its relative cost is lessened and thereby increasing demand and freeing up capital for alternative uses (Jeavons, 1865). This is a key reason why the ability of efficiency strategies to successfully address the crisis in society-nature relations is likely to remain limited.

Green Growth in Practice

On the one hand, energy efficiency measures have been adopted in different sectors by a large number of countries. Mandatory efficiency regulation on final energy consumption has reached almost 25% in 2014 (IEA, 2015). Indeed, primary energy intensity has declined in 80% of surveyed countries since 2014 through different measures such as energy efficiency programs and regulations, GHG regulations and transformation of economic activities (WEC, 2016). Primary energy intensity has improved in all regions of the world in the last two decades (ESCAP, UNEP, UNU & IGES, 2016). However, even though energy efficiency and clean energy have led to significant improvements in carbon intensity, there has been a sharp increase in global emissions, particularly in rapidly developing countries. This is because improvements in energy efficiency have not been sufficient to offset the rapid economic growth in emerging economies. For example, even though China reduced carbon emissions from fuel combustion per unit of GDP by 55% between 1990 and 2011, its emissions per capita tripled in the same period, and are now larger than the EU27 average, even though China is still much poorer (Hoffmann, 2016). The Republic of Korea, the main proponent of green growth, has also more than doubled its emissions per capita in the same period, though efficiency of carbon emissions from fuel combustion per unit of GDP increased by more than 8% in the same period. Indeed, South Korea's National Strategy for Green Growth and Five-Year Plan for Green Growth revealed by former president Lee was criticized for being based on nuclear energy expansion, land reclamation, canal cutting and dredging, and the construction of a multitude of dams and weirs—all of which would place further strain upon the country's beleaguered natural environment. It was little surprise when Lee's initiatives faced a barrage of criticism, and that the subsequent governments, under President Geun-hye Park, considered "ditching" green growth altogether (Shin, 2013).

Green growth is not expected to change the high growth in energy demand in emerging economies expected until 2040 (IEA, 2015). In order to offset emissions to reach the goals of the Paris Agreement (less than 2°C increase in average temperature), the rate of decarbonisation needs to reach 6.3% per annum until 2100; in contrast the achieved rate in 2016, despite a marked improvement over historical rates (0.8% between 2000 and 2011) was 2.6% (PricewaterhouseCoopers LLP, 2017). The future of this trend is unclear, at best. For instance, improvement in energy efficiency seems to have weakened recently: its annual rate declined from 1.6% between 2000 and 2008 to 1.3% since then (WEC, 2016).

[…]

Conclusion

The language of green growth is alluring for a political economy mired in lingering economic lethargy, persistent poverty, rising inequality and stubborn environmental crises that persist and expand despite four decades of modern environmentalism. Collectively, these crises have undermined confidence in economic orthodoxy's assertion that growth is good, even necessary. Greening growth, thus, is a promise to heal that distrust—growth is good because it can be "green." In practice, however, this proposal has not withstood scrutiny. It holds an excessively narrow, even contrived, notion that technological efficiency (enabled through surplus from economic growth) amounts to ameliorating the cumulative and continuing social and ecological impacts of economic growth orthodoxy. Green growth projects have turned to authoritarian politics in pursuit of investments in heavy infrastructure projects and thereby undermining the very institutional foundations of democratic decision-making long recognized in the sustainable development literature. What is apparent to dispassionate inquiry is the limited nature of ecological modernization strategies, be they authoritarian or democratic.

The democratic version is necessary, but insufficient to redress our present crises. Acknowledging this evidence, many civil society actors across the world are instead in pursuit of alternatives to economic orthodoxy. They have advanced alternatives that organize labour and control over consumption and production in ways that attempt re-embedding the economic system within society. These movements to counter the orthodoxy's arrangement of situating the economy in an autonomous and controlling position over society are foundational. They appear to proceed through resistance, innovation but also through accommodation. The path ahead is yet unclear but the goal is less so. Despite current ambiguity they are fertile and urgent grounds for innovation, experimentation and social change.

References

1. Bluemling, B., & Yun S-J. (2016). Giving green teeth to the Tiger? A critique of green growth in South Korea. In Dale, G., Mathai, M. V. and Puppim de Oliveira, J. A. (Eds.), *Green Growth: Ideology, Political Economy and the Alternatives* (pp. 114-130). London: Zed Books.
2. Böhm, S., Misoczky, M.C.A., Watson, D. & Lanka, S. (2016). Alternatives to green growth? Possibilities and contradictions of self-managed food production. In Dale, G.; Mathai, M. V. and

Puppim de Oliveira, J. A. (Eds.), *Green Growth: Ideology, Political Economy and the Alternatives* (pp. 253-269). London: Zed Books.

3. Dale, G., Mathai, M. V. and Puppim de Oliveira, J. A. (Eds.) (2016). *Green Growth: Ideology, Political Economy and the Alternatives* (pp. 90-111). London: Zed Books.

4. Down to Earth (1993). Chipko: Environmentalism of the Poor. Retrieved 11 August 2017, from: http://www.downtoearth.org.in/news/chipko-environmentalism-of-the-poor-30899

5. ESCAP, UNEP, UNU and IGES (2016). *Transformations for Sustainable Development: Promoting Environmental Sustainability in Asia and the Pacific.* Report edited by ESCAP, UNEP, UNU and IGES. Retrieved 16 November 2016, from http://www.unescap.org/publications/transformation-for-sdg

6. Hoffmann, U. (2016). Can green growth really work? A reality check that elaborates on the true (socio-) economics of climate change. In Dale, G., Mathai, M. V. and Puppim de Oliveira, J. A. (Eds.), *Green Growth: Ideology, Political Economy and the Alternatives* (pp. 22-41). London: Zed Books.

7. IEA—International Energy Agency (2015). *World Energy Outlook* (WEO 2015). IEA: Paris.

8. Jeavons, W. S. (1865). *The Coal Question: An Inquiry Concerning the Progress of the Nation and the Probable Exhaustion of Our Coal-Mines.* London and Cambridge: McMillan and Co.

9. Kothari, A. (2016). Beyond "development" and "growth": The search for alternatives in India towards a sustainable and equitable world. In Dale, G., Mathai, M. V. and Puppim de Oliveira, J. A. (Eds.), *Green Growth: Ideology, Political Economy and the Alternatives* (pp. 212-232). London: Zed Books.

10. Lohmann, L. (2016). What is the "green" in "green growth"? In Dale, G., Mathai, M. V. and Puppim de Oliveira, J. A. (Eds.), *Green Growth: Ideology, Political Economy and the Alternatives* (pp. 42-71). London: Zed Books.

11. Mahnkopf, B. (2016). Lessons from the EU: Why capitalism cannot be rescued from its own contradictions. In Dale, G., Mathai, M. V. and Puppim de Oliveira, J. A. (Eds.), *Green Growth:*

Ideology, Political Economy and the Alternatives (pp. 131-149). London: Zed Books.

12. Martinez-Alier, J., Demaria, F., Temper, L., & Walter, M. (2016). Trends of social metabolism and environmental conflict: A comparison between India and Latin America. In Dale, G., Mathai, M. V. and Puppim de Oliveira, J. A. (Eds.), *Green Growth: Ideology, Political Economy and the Alternatives* (pp. 187-210). London: Zed Books.

13. Meadway, J. (2016). Degrowth and the roots of neoclassical economics. In Dale, G., Mathai, M. V. and Puppim de Oliveira, J. A. (Eds.), *Green Growth: Ideology, Political Economy and the Alternatives* (pp. 90-111). London: Zed Books.

14. Pickett, K., & Wilkinson, R. (2009). *The Spirit Level: Why more equal societies almost always do better.* London: Allen Lane.

15. PricewaterhouseCoopers LLP (2017). *Is Paris Possible? The Low Carbon Economy Index 2017.* Retrieved 7 April 2018, from https://www.pwc.co.uk/sustainability-climate-change/assets/pdf/lcei-17-pdf-final-v2.pdf

16. Rockstrom, J., Steffen, W., Noone, K., Persson, Å., Chapin III, F.S., Lambin, E.F., Lenton, T.M., Scheffer, M., Folke, C., Schellnhuber, H.J., Nykvist, B., de Wit, C.A., Hughes, T., van der Leeuw, S., Rodhe, H., Sörlin, S., Snyder, P.K., Costanza, R., Svedin, U., Falken-mark, M., Karlberg, L., Corell, R.W., Fabry, V.J., Hansen, J., Walker, B.H., Liverman, D., Richardson, K., Crutzen, P. & Foley, J.A. (2009). A Safe Operating Space for Humanity. *Nature*, 461, 472–475.

17. Rogers, H. (2010). *Green Gone Wrong: How our economy is undermining the environmental revolution.* New York: Simon and Schuster.

18. Shin, Hyon-hee (2013). South Korea ditching green growth. The Korea Herald (online). Published in the Asia News Network. Retrieved 27 August 2013, from www.asianewsnet.net/South-Korea-ditching-green-growth-44753.html

19. Smith, Adam (1993 [1776]). *The Wealth of Nations.* Oxford: Oxford University Press.

20. Smith, R. (2014, January 15). Beyond Growth or Beyond Capitalism? *Truthout.* Retrieved 12 March 2015, from http://

www.truth-out.org/news/item/21215-beyond-growth-or-beyond-capitalism#

21. Stiglitz, J. E., Sen, A. and Fitoussi, J-P (2009). Report by the Commission on the Measurement of Economic Performance and Social Progress. Retrieved 6 November 2016, from http://www.stiglitz-sen-fitoussi.fr/documents/rapport_anglais.pdf

22. Sunderlin, William (2003). *Ideology, Social Theory and the Environment*. Lanham, MD: Rowman & Littlefield.

23. Taminiau, J., & Byrne, J. (2016). Reconsidering growth in the greenhouse: The Sustainable Energy Utility (SEU) as a practical strategy for the twenty-first century. In Dale, G., Mathai, M. V. and Puppim de Oliveira, J. A. (Eds.), *Green Growth: Ideology, Political Economy and the Alternatives* (pp. 233-252). London: Zed Books.

24. Tierney, J. (2009, April 20). Use energy, get rich and save the planet. *The New York Times*. Retrieved 25 May 2011, from http://www.nytimes.com/2009/04/21/science/earth/21tier.html

25. World Bank (2017). World GDP per capita growth (annual %). Retrieved 11 August 2017, from http://data.worldbank.org/indicator/NY.GDP.PCAP.KD.ZG

26. WEC-World Energy Council (2016). *World Energy Perspectives Energy Efficiency: A Straight Path Towards Energy Sustainability*. London: The World Energy Council in partnership with ADEME.

VIEWPOINT 4

> "The Green New Deal is a piece of public policy that is carefully crafted to address the interrelated crises of environmental degradation and social inequality."

A Green New Deal Makes Economic Sense

Sophie Carter

In the following excerpted viewpoint, Sophie Carter argues that the Green New Deal bill from Rep. Alexandria Ocasio-Cortez and Sen. Ed Markey would benefit both the environment and the US economy at a time of crisis. Carter lays groundwork by explaining the dire situation regarding climate change and enumerates ways in which the Green New Deal could address it. She adds that the legislation also would create jobs and lift many Americans out of poverty by providing them with fair wages. Sophie Carter is a political opinions columnist for The Heights.

As you read, consider the following questions:

1. How does the climate crisis highlight social inequities?
2. If the Green New Deal is non-binding, then why is the author optimistic about it?
3. How many new green jobs could be created by this bill, according to the author?

"A Green New Deal Makes Economic and Environmental Sense," by Sophie Carter, *The Heights*, April 25, 2021. Reprinted by permission.

Last Tuesday, U.S. Representative Alexandria Ocasio-Cortez of New York and Massachusetts' own U.S. Senator Ed Markey took the ambitious steps to formally reintroduce their signature bill, the Green New Deal. With new Democratic control of both houses of Congress and the White House, it appears as though the most sweeping piece of climate legislation in history may have another chance at being passed. If so, it will transform the national economic and environmental landscape. It is well past time for the Democratic Party to uniformly rally around the Green New Deal and work to change the course of climate injustice in America.

As it stands today, climate change is undoubtedly one of the most pressing issues facing the world. There are concerning signs surrounding the prospects for maintaining an inhabitable world—storms and major weather events are worsening, the sea level is rising, and humans have already warmed the globe by about one degree Celsius.

It is also important to note that the effects of the climate and environmental crises are not uniformly felt across all social groups. Declining air and water quality is far more likely to impact racial minorities, especially those who live in urban areas. In the United States, one out of every six Black children suffer from asthma due to poor air quality, and they are five times more likely than white children to contract lead poisoning because they live in close proximity to toxic waste. On a more global scale, the majority of those who will be displaced by rising sea levels, unstable weather events, and plummeting food supplies will be those who live in developing nations, mostly in the global south. It is evident that this situation is fundamentally unfair and unsustainable. The question is, what can we do about this moral and environmental crisis?

The Green New Deal is a piece of public policy that is carefully crafted to address the interrelated crises of environmental degradation and social inequality. Scientists agree that in order to achieve a best-case scenario surrounding the changing climate, the world needs to achieve carbon neutrality by the year 2050. The Green New Deal aims to push the U.S. to take on a leading role in working toward this goal by implementing a 10-year plan that includes investing in the move to 100 percent renewable energy and sustainable infrastructure. All of these goals would be achieved through creating high-paying, green jobs in order to reduce economic inequality and retrain those who work in the dying fossil fuel industry. Although the bill would function as a non-binding resolution, its passage would signal national cohesion on climate-friendly initiatives that are already being implemented at state and local levels.

In addition to being a comprehensive and innovative piece of public policy, the Green New Deal makes economic sense. Climate change is both a threat to our existence and a fantastic opportunity to rebuild our economy in an equitable and sustainable manner. It is helpful to view the Green New Deal as more of an investment than anything else—if Congress is bold in its climate action, it could create an estimated 10.6 million new green jobs, expand job training for skilled laborers, and revitalize the role of unions in protecting American workers. By investing in sustainable infrastructure and labor, sweeping legislation could put millions of people to work with fair wages and jumpstart a post-pandemic economy, functioning to lift people out of poverty and rebuild the middle class. By shrinking income inequality and the influence of environmental racism, we could make our new green economy open to everyone.

Despite the benefits that would be achieved by addressing economic inequality and climate change, the Green New Deal has become a polarizing force in American politics. The objections to the Green New Deal are largely predictable. Republicans in government decry the so-called presence of socialism, relying on straw man arguments that incite fear around absurdities like the possibility of Democrats banning hamburgers and milkshakes. Moderate Democrats also exhibit reticence towards taking such bold action out of fear of shutting down the possibility of bipartisanship, but these legislators desperately need a reality check. Bipartisan cooperation on climate is a non-starter, and one needs to look no further for evidence than the bad-faith claims by Republicans that "airplanes will be banned" under Democratic climate leadership. Compromise is not likely on this issue, no matter how many concessions Democratic lawmakers make. That is simply a reality that Democrats need to accept, and they should not let this fear of acting in a partisan manner stop them from implementing an economically and environmentally sound piece of legislation.

Incrementalism will inevitably fail to adequately tackle the monumental task of moving the country toward carbon neutrality, and the communities affected by environmental injustice deserve better than baby steps in the right direction. It's time for the Democratic Party to muster its political courage and continue to shift the way we talk about climate change, inequality, and environmental racism, and the best way to do this is by passing the Green New Deal.

Periodical and Internet Sources Bibliography

The following articles have been selected to supplement the diverse views presented in this chapter.

Nafeez Ahmed, "Green Economic Growth Is a Myth," Vice, July 16, 2021, https://www.vice.com/en/article/qj4z9p/green-economic-growth-is-a-myth.

Spencer Bokat-Lindell, "Do We Need to Shrink the Economy to Stop Climate Change?" *New York Times*, September 16, 2021, https://www.nytimes.com/2021/09/16/opinion/degrowth-cllimate-change.html.

Mirek Dusek, "Business Leaders Embrace Europe's New Green Reality for Investment and Growth," World Economic Forum, September 16, 2021, https://www.weforum.org/agenda/2020/09/business-leaders-embrace-europe-s-new-green-reality-for-investment-and-growth.

Gregory Krieg, Laura Dolan, and Jason Carroll, "The Green Energy Revolution Is Coming—With or Without Help from Washington," CNN Politics, June 10, 2021, https://www.cnn.com/2021/06/10/politics/green-energy-infrastructure-electric-grid/index.html.

Robinson Meyer, "How the U.S. Made Progress on Climate Change Without Ever Passing a Bill," *The Atlantic*, June 16, 2021, https://www.theatlantic.com/science/archive/2021/06/climate-change-green-vortex-america/619228.

George Monbiot, "Green Growth Doesn't Exist—Less of Everything Is the Only Way to Avert Catastrophe," *The Guardian*, September 29, 2021, https://www.theguardian.com/commentisfree/2021/sep/29/green-growth-economic-activity-environment.

Steven Mufson, "A Surge in Green Financing Boosts Climate Businesses," *Washington Post*, January 27, 2021, https://www.washingtonpost.com/climate-solutions/2021/01/27/surge-green-financing-boosts-climate-businesses.

Noam Scheiber, "Can a Green-Economy Boom Town Be Built to Last?" *New York Times*, September 13, 2021, https://www.nytimes.com/2021/09/13/business/rivian-illinois-electric-vehicles.html.

CHAPTER 4

Is a Green Economy Beneficial to American Businesses and Investors?

Chapter Preface

One of the most important areas of debate on climate and environmental policy concerns the potential impact of green reform on the business and investment environment. Both consumers and investors are increasingly aware of climate change and its associated risks and have demonstrated a growing desire to work with companies that are participating in the movement toward a greener, more sustainable economy. New business ideas have emerged as part of the green economy movement, including subscription-based energy programs, mine reclamation projects, and energy service companies (ESCOs). And business leaders have begun to pay attention to the long-term benefits that their companies can derive from short-term investments in efficiency and sustainability. BCG consultants Shalini Unnikrishnan, Chris Biggs, and Nidhi Singh detail some of the potential long-term benefits of such investments:

> Sustainability is not an add-on. It's about building competitive advantage, lowering risk, getting ahead of new regulations, gaining ground with investors, and adjusting to new consumer demands. And companies can get a better return on investment from the operational and supply chain changes that are already being made by embedding sustainability within those changes. A sustainability focus also builds resilience—although the link between sustainability and resilience was already evident, it has become even clearer during the pandemic. For companies, all this flows back into long-term success.[1]

The benefits of sustainable investment and other green strategies have become increasingly clear to the business community as a whole. But many investors and business leaders are wary of green reform because they associate the environmental movement with excessive and burdensome regulations. Moreover, investors and managers are generally attracted to predictability, and innovation is inherently riskier than many other business activities. The small business community faces a particularly vexing set of challenges when it comes to managing the transition to a green economy. These challenges include costly access to external financing, a limited capacity for diversification, and a variety of other size-related constraints. Some business experts have argued that an expansive, macro-level policy package like the Green New Deal would establish a clear new direction for the global economy and give investors the confidence necessary to jump into the green economy with both feet.

The viewpoints in this chapter represent a variety of perspectives in the debate about how to manage the impact of green reform on the business and investment environment in the United States.

Notes

1. "Sustainability Matters Now More Than Ever for Consumer Companies," by Shalini Unnikrishnan, Chris Biggs, and Nidhi Singh, The Boston Consulting Group, August 11, 2020. Reprinted by permission. https://www.bcg.com/en-in/publications/2020/sustainability-matters-now-more-than-ever-for-consumer-companies

VIEWPOINT 1

> "An industrial green policy in the spirit of the Green New Deal with the goal of solving climate change would spur massive amounts of innovation, new markets, and businesses—a vast opportunity for investors."

Investors Should Embrace the Scope and Scale of the Green New Deal

Daniel Stewart

In the following viewpoint, Daniel Stewart presents a case that the scope and scale of the Green New Deal is precisely what is needed to encourage businesses and investors to participate enthusiastically in the movement toward a green economy. He begins by reviewing the alarming scientific conclusions in the 2018 IPCC Special Report on Global Warming and pointing out the risks that investors would face if the global community fails to respond decisively. The problem at the moment, according to Stewart, is that businesses and investors are unsure of what to expect from their governments in the years ahead, given the unpredictability of politics in recent years. He suggests that an expansive, macro-level policy package like the Green New Deal would establish a clear new direction for the global economy and give investors the confidence necessary to jump into the green economy with both feet. Daniel Stewart is a sustainability consultant and climate program manager for As You Sow, a shareholder advocacy nonprofit that promotes environmental and human rights goals.

"A Green New Deal Is a Smart Deal for Investors," by Daniel Stewart, As You Sow, July 30, 2019. Reprinted by permission.

As you read, consider the following questions:

1. Why should investors and portfolio managers be concerned about the effects of climate change?
2. If US policymakers fail to act decisively on climate change, how will that affect the United States' competitive advantage in the global green economy?
3. Why does Stewart believe that it is important for investors to be vocal about their interest in climate policy and green reform?

In recent months, the Green New Deal has sparked a movement centered on the need for bold action on climate. So what is this Green New Deal and why are investors supporting it?

In February 2019, representative Alexandria Ocasio-Cortez (NY-14) and Senator Edward Markey (MA) introduced the Green New Deal as a non-binding resolution. The resolution lays out an ambitious federal strategy to decarbonize the U.S. economy and thereby increase clean power, create good jobs, improve air and water quality, while increasing U.S. global competitiveness. The carbon reduction goals of the Green New Deal are informed by the scientific consensus about the increasing impacts of global warming as set forth in the latest report, Special Report on Global Warming of 1.5°C, by the Intergovernmental Panel on Climate Change (IPCC) released in the fall of 2018. The Green New Deal concept is not new, but it is gaining clarity and momentum and has catapulted climate change to the forefront of national dialogue at a critical time.

The IPCC report states that we have a narrowing window in which to act to avoid catastrophic climate impacts. Global human-caused greenhouse gas emissions need to fall nearly 50 percent from 2010 levels by 2030 and decline to "net zero" around 2050. "Net zero" requires emissions to drop essentially to zero and any remaining emissions must be balanced by removing CO_2 or other greenhouse gases from the air. The IPCC report projects an alarming difference in global impacts between limiting warming to 1.5°C versus 2°C and beyond.

The effects of climate change are complex and unpredictable but are understood to be incredibly destructive and harmful to the stability of the global environmental systems upon which human society and the economy depend. Climate impacts present broad portfolio risks to investors who hold interests in companies and industries across all sectors of the global economy. Awareness of the systemic risk that climate change poses to the global economy is developing in influential institutions. For example, the Network for Greening the Financial System, a coalition of 36 central banks, was established at the end of 2017 with the purpose of helping to achieve the goals of the Paris Agreement and manage risks to the financial system. Frank Elderson, chair of the Network for Greening the Financial System, forcefully stated that "a transition to a green and low-carbon economy is not a niche nor is it a 'nice to have' for the happy few. It is crucial for our own survival. There is no alternative."

Letting the current "business as usual" approach run its course is going to be devastatingly costly for investors. Recent research has put the costs of inaction at trillions of dollars. A report by CDP showed that, based on companies' self-reported analyses, climate change could cost a combined total of almost $1 trillion, with much of this occurring in the coming five years. The companies accounted for in the report represent only a slice of the market; the report does not count major corporations with outsized risk like oil and gas giants Chevron and Exxon, which have refused to disclose critical climate-related data to CDP.

An industrial green policy in the spirit of the Green New Deal with the goal of solving climate change would spur massive amounts of innovation, new markets, and businesses—a vast opportunity for investors. According to economist Mariana Mazzucato, director of the Institute for Innovation and Public Purpose in University College London, a Green New Deal "should create new opportunities for investment, so that growth and sustainability move hand in hand."

The shift toward a decarbonized global economy is already happening. The issue now is the pace of transformation. China and the European Union are positioning themselves as leaders in innovation for the emerging zero-carbon economy. The longer the U.S. procrastinates, the more it will suffer missed opportunities and resultant economic consequences. Just think of who will dominate the solar and wind markets, the emerging energy storage market, the electric vehicle market, and all the untold products and services needed to decarbonize the rest of the economy. While China introduces policy to support clean energy vehicles, the U.S. is attempting to roll back fuel efficiency standards to benefit oil companies and car manufacturers.

A truism of markets is that business does not invest unless it sees an opportunity for growth. The Green New Deal would spur market opportunity. By clearly establishing that this is the direction our country is headed, corporations would be better able to plan for necessary change, secure competitive advantage, respond to new opportunities, and mitigate against the risks posed by climate change. Such policies would not only help in limiting climate related risk but also create an abundance of opportunity for the investment community. Recent research projects a potential direct economic gain of $26tn by 2030 if bold climate action is taken. Nobel-prize winning economist Joseph Stiglitz has endorsed the idea of a Green New Deal touting that it would be good for the economy by stimulating demand, creating jobs, and likely ushering in a new economic boom.

Given what a Green New Deal could do to protect and unlock future value in investor portfolios, what can the investment community do to support its core principles? Investors must be vocal about what they have to lose and gain in face of the growing climate crisis and must support the solutions needed to prevent massive value destruction. Investor support for the concepts embedded in the Green New Deal is clearly growing. This was recently demonstrated by an investor letter organized by *As You Sow* with support from more than 50 investors representing more than $60 billion in assets under management. The letter was sent to every representative and senator on the 116th congress, urging action. Investors must also incorporate this urgent message into engagements with corporations. *As You Sow*'s 2019 resolution with oil and gas company Chevron, for example, calls for the company to explain how it can align its business model with the Paris Agreement—a request very much in line with what the Green New Deal aims to achieve. Investors must ensure that the companies in which they invest provide information to understand the risk and opportunity their business actions are creating and have a clearly communicated vision for how they will align with Paris net zero targets.

Finally, investors should reflect on their own investment strategy. As mentioned previously, central banks and financial regulators are becoming more acutely aware of the risk and corresponding financial materiality of climate change. As such, the fiduciary duty of investors regarding climate change is under scrutiny. Recently a panel of financial experts from Harvard, Stanford, and other respected institutions advising the New York State Common Retirement Fund concluded that "the fund pursue alignment of its entire portfolio with a 2-degree or lower future by 2030 in accordance with the climate science consensus." This view is similar to *As You Sow*'s call in a 2018 report—2020: A Clear Vision for Paris Compliant Shareholder Engagement—calling on investors to ensure that the oil and gas companies in which they invest have low carbon business transition plans in place to help ensure alignment with the Paris Agreement goals of keeping global warming at or near 1.5°C.

Ultimately, the ethos of the Green New Deal should be embraced and supported by investors. If carried out comprehensively, it would bring about ambitious policy solutions commensurate with the magnitude of the climate change emergency, create a clear pathway forward to protect investment interests, transform and decarbonize the U.S. economy, minimize risk of climate breakdown impacts, and maximize opportunities in the low-carbon economy.

VIEWPOINT 2

> "Businesses can create a profitable competitive advantage by adopting one or more of the GND's concepts. For example, companies in California and Hawaii are pioneering solar battery farms."

Investors Can Take Advantage of the Green New Deal

Michael Kahn

In the following viewpoint, Michael Kahn discusses how the investment community can prepare for and take advantage of the business opportunities that would result from a major climate policy package like the Green New Deal. He identifies key industries that are well-positioned for growth in the green economy and points to a number of areas where new business models could find traction. He also suggests that the ultimate outcome of the GND policy debate is less important than the impact of the proposal on the public conversation. The growing popularity of green reform will encourage new market opportunities regardless of what policies are eventually implemented. Michael Kahn is a chartered market technician and a contributing writer at Kiplinger.com. His work has been featured in Barron's Online, MarketWatch, and the Nightly Business Report.

"What the Green New Deal Means for Investors," by Michael Kahn, The Kiplinger Washington Editors, Inc., June 7, 2019. Reprinted by permission. Copyright 2019 The Kiplinger Washington Editors, Inc.

Is a Green Economy Beneficial to American Businesses and Investors?

As you read, consider the following questions:

1. Why does the author suggest that the growing mainstream popularity of the Green New Deal concept may be more important for investors than the policy details?
2. What are some of the things that investors should look for in companies to determine their competitive prospects in the green economy?
3. Which industries does the author identify as being especially well-positioned to grow in the green economy of the future?

The Green New Deal (GND) is a plan to drastically change the American economy and improve social conditions for its people. It was put forth in March by Rep. Alexandria Ocasio-Cortez (D-N.Y.) and Sen. Ed Markey (D-Mass.) but stalled in Congress after a Senate defeat. However, the GND still is a topic of wide debate and already has spawned various copycat proposals—and its underlying movement still will have a significant effect on the economy and investors going forward.

Modeled after FDR's New Deal in 1933 but focusing on fighting climate change, the Green New Deal is controversial for several reasons, including its enormous cost and rapid timetable.

I am not going to argue politics today. But while some, most or even all of the proposal may never be passed into law, there is no denying that the trend toward a more Earth-friendly economy is in place. A few states already have long-term 100% renewable-energy mandates in places, and literally hundreds of mayors and several governors have expressed support in 100% goals.

With or without the GND, some technologies—such as electric vehicles, solar power and ocean-friendly packaging—will develop into viable industries.

This presents many opportunities for investors. The question is where should they put their money, assuming that at least the underlying concepts within the Green New Deal materialize?

Why Go Green?

Again, without even discussing whether the GND is possible, viable or even desirable, we can at least stipulate that being more environmentally friendly is desirable. Being a better shepherd to the planet, protecting ecosystems and using natural resources wisely make sense for the simple reason that clean air, water, food and even recreational facilities are good for all of us.

The No. 1 "green" issue for most people is climate change caused by emissions of carbon dioxide and other so-called greenhouse gasses. In the atmosphere, these gases trap heat and raise the average temperature around the world.

According to the United Nations' World Meteorological Organization, the average global temperature is on track to increase by 5.4 to 9.0 degrees Fahrenheit through the end of the century.

That doesn't sound like much, especially when the average high and low temperatures in a city such as New York vary 57 degrees from winter to summer and can swing from single to triple digits at their extremes. But that seemingly little range is all it takes to drastically shift weather patterns, causing stronger storms and altering crops, sea levels and rainfall.

With the public now increasingly aware of climate change and roughly three-quarters of Americans "somewhat" or "very worried" about it, according to a poll from Yale University, George Mason University and Climate Nexus, investors should be mindful of the companies that will directly benefit from fighting it.

The Basics of the Green New Deal

In a nutshell, the GND seeks to:

1. Shift 100% of national power generation to renewable source within 10 years. Initially, it sought a zero-emission target but it has since been changed to "net zero." That means carbon emissions from natural sources, such as the decay of organic materials, would be harnessed to provide power first before being emitted. In 2017, only 11% of the nation's energy consumption came from renewables, according to the Energy Information Administration. Another 9%

is generated by nuclear power. Although not renewable, nuclear doesn't emit carbon dioxide.

2. Upgrade all buildings to make them energy-efficient. This means replacing all building infrastructure to eliminate heating oil and natural gas. It also means replacing all electric air conditioners that use HFC refrigerants (hydrofluorocarbons), which are 2,000 times more potent than carbon dioxide as greenhouse gasses.

3. Decarbonize manufacturing and agricultural industries. Infrastructure would be required to "scrub" emissions to remove carbon. It also is where "cow emissions" can be captured to provide energy.

4. Decarbonize and upgrade the nation's infrastructure, especially transportation, specifically shifting nonessential individual transportation to mass transit. While high-speed rail was suggested as a preferred method for domestic travel, it was not true that the plan called for rail travel on overseas routes.

5. Fund massive investment in the drawdown and capture of greenhouse gases. Technology to recapture carbon from the air would have to be developed.

6. As a byproduct, the U.S. could become a major exporter of green technology, products and expertise.

7. Guarantee jobs for those who are vocationally displaced by these changes

8. Guaranteed minimum income and universal healthcare.

Surprisingly, the Green New Deal does not include a carbon tax or a cap-and-trade program. These programs, which essentially shift the cost of polluting from one organization to another, raise the cost of carbon fuels, such as gasoline. That could hurt lower-income families more, especially those in rural areas who rely on an automobile.

Economic Impact

The obvious theme for investors is to put their money in companies that are already making inroads toward a greener economy. This could be through adoption of renewable power, electric vehicles, which includes cars, trains, trucks and even airplanes, and the development of new technologies to recapture carbon, either at the source or from the air.

Finding specific investments will require a bit more work and thinking on a more micro level.

Jobs in industries that would be restricted or eliminated, such as oil and gas drillers and refiners, would disappear unless they're easily adaptable to new green-energy industries. Energy costs for home heating and electric power would likely double or triple, according to a Heritage Foundation study—and that's only at a 50% adoption of renewable fuels. Therefore, building heating and cooling would be an important area for innovation.

Utilities would have to shift their power-generation mix away from coal and fossil fuels and toward renewables. This is happening to some extent already—the U.S. Energy Information Administration says that last year, "renewable energy sources accounted for about 11% of total U.S. energy consumption and about 17% of electricity generation." But a full migration would come at great cost and threaten gas utilities dramatically, unless they can deliver biogas and hydrogen gas.

However, jobs in new industries that create store and distribute clean power would flourish. This includes manufacturers of electric and battery-powered autos and components, home heating and cooling, carbon-recovery devices and "green" consulting.

Employee retraining programs and education would grow. Universal healthcare would end private insurance companies—at least as we know them.

Businesses can create a profitable competitive advantage by adopting one or more of the GND's concepts. For example, companies in California and Hawaii are pioneering solar battery farms. And the price of wind and solar energy continues to fall, making it more competitive with fossil fuels today. Nonpartisan think tank Energy Innovation says "local wind and solar could replace approximately 74 percent of the U.S. coal fleet at an immediate savings to customers."

In short, companies that are ahead of the curve in adopting renewable energy will have a significant advantage over those that are behind.

Areas for Investment

Kenneth Ameduri—chief editor and co-founder of CrushTheStreet.com, an alternative financial and economic news website—suggests lightening up on the traditional energy and utilities sectors and moving toward companies in the sustainable energy sector. His favorites include clean power generation asset company TerraForm Power (TERP, $13.60), biodiesel-focused company Renewable Energy Group (REGI, $14.09) and Spain's Siemens Gamesa Renewable Energy SA (GCTAF, $16.04), one of the world's largest producers of wind turbines.

It doesn't matter whether the Green New Deal or similar legislation passes, he says, "because the seeds have been planted in the minds of the public, which in turn will have an impact on the markets."

The best-known source of renewable energy is solar power. Austin Vincent, analyst at the Memphis-based hedge fund Gullane Capital Partners, thinks First Solar (FSLR, $61.42) will be a top choice. First Solar manufactures utility-scale solar panels and should become of strategic importance to U.S. interests, given that the alternative is replacing domestic oil and gas infrastructure with Chinese-made solar panels.

Again, the strategy for investors is to find stocks and other securities that are already complying with the trend toward a greener planet.

The Green New Deal, if ever enacted in some shape or form, would only accelerate what is already coming our way.

VIEWPOINT 3

> "Without sufficient financial incentives and technical support, small businesses could be less willing to invest in green technologies. There is a risk that small businesses will be left behind in climate transition."

Green Reform Poses a Unique Set of Challenges for Small Business

Addisu Lashitew

In the following viewpoint, Addisu Lashitew looks specifically at the challenges facing the small business community in the wake of the COVID-19 pandemic and how those challenges affect small businesses' ability to participate in the transition to a greener economy. These challenges include costly access to external financing, a limited capacity for diversification relative to larger firms, and a variety of other size-related constraints. He argues that the Small Business Green Recovery Fund in the Biden administration's Build Back Better proposal offers an effective model for how policymakers can help the small business community manage these challenges. Addisu Lashitew is a nonresident fellow in the Global Economy and Development program at the Brookings Institution.

"Small Business Green Recovery Fund to Power US Climate Transition," by Addisu Lashitew, The Brookings Institution, March 1, 2021. Reprinted by permission.

Is a Green Economy Beneficial to American Businesses and Investors?

As you read, consider the following questions:

1. What are some of the reasons why it may be particularly difficult for small businesses to adapt to a green economy?
2. According to the author, how will specialized green funds enhance small businesses' ability to invest in sustainability and energy efficiency?
3. Why did the COVID-19 pandemic have a greater impact on small businesses than on larger, more established companies?

The U.S. private sector faces the twin challenges of recovering from the devastating effects of the pandemic and transitioning to a low-carbon economy. The Biden administration's plan for "building back better" underscores the need to support small businesses and advance racial equity, to which it has proposed a $30 billion Small Business Opportunity Fund. There is, however, a need for cross-cutting policy initiatives that exploit the unique opportunity presented by the pandemic to simultaneously advance sustainability and rapid economic recovery. This proposal calls for a $50 billion federal "Small Business Green Recovery Fund" that promotes green innovations and investments among small businesses that advance climate change mitigation, adaptation, and other sustainability solutions.

The fund will cater to the diverse financial needs of small businesses by offering financial support in the form of green grants, green loans, and green bonds. The green grants scheme aims to bolster the ability of the Small Business Administration to support green innovations and investments to small businesses that face limited and costly access to financial markets. The remaining components of the Fund are to be channeled on a commercial basis through intermediary financial institutions by building on the experiences of the Paycheck Protection and the Mainstreet Lending Programs. The green loans scheme will provide financing for green projects that small businesses would otherwise struggle to implement due to their high upfront and borrowing costs. The green bonds scheme will avail financing for green bond issuances by small and medium financial institutions that offer climate financing for small businesses. Identification of green projects that are eligible for funding, and assessment and verification of their environmental impacts will be based on decentralized, market-based screening and verification protocols. Overall, the proposed Fund will boost competitiveness and sustainable recovery, simultaneously contributing to the Biden administration's multipronged agenda to advance racial equity and inclusion, to revitalize American industries ("Made in all of America"), and to achieve carbon neutrality by 2050 through "clean energy revolution and environmental justice."

Challenge

Small businesses with 500 or fewer employees numbered 30.2 million in 2018, making up 99.9 percent of the total number of businesses in the U.S. They employed 58.9 million workers,[1] equivalent to 47.5 percent of the U.S. workforce, and contributed to 43.5 percent of non-farm GDP in 2014.[2] They also registered faster growth, paid higher wages, and contributed to 30 percent of total merchandise exports. Just above 28 percent of small businesses were owned by minorities and 33 percent by women in 2018, which makes them key drivers of inclusion and local economic growth. The vast majority of them operate in services industries such as real estate, accommodation and food services, wholesale and retail trade, construction, and professional services, where they contribute to at least to half of total employment.[3]

Estimates from OECD economies with similar economic structures to the U.S suggest that small businesses contribute to 60-70 percent of total industrial pollution. Achieving climate transition will thus require new investments and technological innovations to overhaul production processes, consumption patterns, and supply chain linkages in the small business ecosystem. The Biden administration's plan to achieve 100 percent clean energy and net-zero emissions by 2050 is thus unlikely to be met without measures that incentivize small businesses to make these investments. Climate transition can also provide businesses with vast growth opportunities through innovations and investments that improve energy efficiency and by providing access to the growing market for sustainable goods and services. One of the goals of climate policy should hence be enabling small businesses to get ahead of the climate transition curve to take advantage of it for improving their productivity, growth, and competitiveness.

The Biden administration's plan to reignite climate transition will face a hurdle in effectively mobilizing small businesses that were disproportionately hurt by the pandemic. From 75-90 percent of small businesses were negatively affected by the precipitous fall of demand in the face of mandatory business closures and social distancing requirements, according to the Small Business Pulse Survey (SBPS) by the U.S. Census Bureau.[4] In late April 2020, 31 percent of small businesses struggled to pay bills, 25 percent were unable to pay rent, 24 percent could not pay wages, and 23 percent failed to meet their debt obligations. These severe effects of the pandemic are also likely to persist, with many small businesses remaining financially weakened and heavily indebted to effectively respond to the climate transition challenge.

Even before the pandemic, the vast majority of small businesses were severely under-prepared to deal with the effects of climate change. Small businesses that have innovative ideas to launch green products often fail to do so, due in part to prohibitively high upfront investments for acquiring capital equipment or developing new technologies. Being young and capital-light, small businesses generally lack credit history and assets that can serve as collateral, which leads to limited and costly access to external financing.[5] Finally, a broad range of size-related constraints creates scale diseconomies for sustainable investments, making it unprofitable for small businesses to invest without financial support. For example, surveys show that energy efficiency investments are less likely to reduce operational costs among small businesses, suggesting the need for financial subsidies to make these investments financially viable.

The combined effect of these constraints is that, without sufficient financial incentives and technical support, small businesses could be less willing to invest in green technologies. Unless climate policy effectively circumvents these disadvantages, there is a risk that small businesses will be left behind in climate transition, which could eventually expose them to greater climate risk and loss of competitiveness. The process could hollow out local economies, increase the market power of large firms, and worsen income inequalities across individuals and communities. If supported by tailored policies to improve their competitiveness, however, small businesses can leverage their agility and innovativeness to become major sources of growth and employment in emerging green industries. A healthy economic recovery will hence require policies that simultaneously revitalize the competitiveness of small businesses and improve their capacity to invest in sustainable solutions.

Limits of Historic and Existing Policies

Small businesses are considered to be risky borrowers with a comparatively greater chance of bankruptcy, which increases their borrowing costs. For green financing initiatives, the additional cost of monitoring and assessing sustainability performance further increases the cost of capital. In many OECD countries, therefore, national and multilateral development banks seek to lower the cost of green financing through various risk-sharing mechanisms such as concessional loans, first-loss investments, and guarantees. For example, the European Investment Bank (EIB), which serves as Europe's climate bank towards meeting COP21 targets, has committed $100 billion to climate-related projects over 2016 -2020.

In contrast, there are no major federal funding programs that provide climate financing for small businesses in the U.S.[6] The Small Business Administration (SBA) and the Treasury have several generic small business financing programs, many of which were introduced or extended to contain economic freefall during the COVID-19 pandemic. The major small business financing programs are described below.

Pre-Pandemic Small Business Funds

The Small Business Lending Program was introduced by the Treasury in 2010 to encourage financial institutions to provide loans for small businesses. Through this program, the Treasury has invested over $4.0 billion in 332 community banks and community development loan funds (CDLFs) since its establishment.

Economic Injury Disaster Loans (EIDL) program provides an upfront advance payment of up to $2 million for small businesses that are unable to meet their debt obligations or pay for their operating expenses due to natural disasters. Funding is provided in a form of loans that can be repaid over a period of up to 30 years. EIDL was vastly expanded to offer relief to businesses affected by the pandemic. By late 2020, it distributed 3.6 million loans with a value of $194 billion—an amount far greater than what the program had given out in its history of 67 years.

State Small Business Credit Initiative (SSBCI) was introduced in 2010 with a funding of $1.5 billion to strengthen state programs that financed small businesses. The Treasury awarded funding to most U.S. states to complement their funding for new or existing state programs through various financing programs.

SBA Grants are several small-scale grants that are administered by the SBA to stimulate small business exporting, innovation, etc.

Post-Pandemic Small Business Funds

Payment Protection Program (PPP) is a part of the CARES Act that is implemented by the Small Business Administration with support from the Department of the Treasury. The PPP was budgeted with $659 billion in forgivable loans for small businesses with 500 or fewer employees. This program provided small businesses with funds to pay for eight to 24 weeks of payroll, mortgages, rent, and utility costs. The program, which ended on August 8, 2020, provided forgivable loans with an interest rate of 1 percent and a maturity of two to five years. The Mainstreet Lending Program, another element of the CARES Act, also provided additional loans of $75 billion for small businesses.

SBA Loan Forgiveness Program exempts small businesses from existing non-disaster SBA loan payments over the period of six months during the pandemic. Beneficiaries are small business owners participating in the agency's various microlending programs.

Proposed legislation titled the Jobs and Neighborhood Investment Act aspires to make a new, $17.9 billion investment in low-income and minority communities that have been hard-hit by the COVID-19 crisis. The legislation intends to provide eligible community development financial institutions (CDFIs) and Minority Depository Institutions (MDIs) with capital, liquidity, and operational capacity to expand the flow of credit to small businesses in underserved, minority, and historically disadvantaged communities.

The financial support programs introduced by the CARES Act have demonstrated how federal assistance can be channeled to contain economic collapse in the face of an unprecedented crisis. However, the programs have also revealed the limits of the approach, which can be taken into account in designing future programs.

First, none of these policies prioritized climate transition, which would require long-term, preferably subsidized, financing schemes. These programs hence represent a missed opportunity for "building back better" by linking economic recovery with climate transition. By contrast, the European Union has set aside 25 percent of its 750 billion euro recovery fund for projects that advance climate transition, and France has likewise dedicated one-third of its 100 billion euro economic stimulus package for green initiatives.[7]

Second, evidence shows that federal assistance during the COVID-19 crisis has been unequally shared. For example, while the PPP managed to reach 5.2 million small businesses by November 2020, just one percent of these borrowers (who received at least

$1.4 million) received more than a quarter of the $523 billion disbursed. This size bias could have a lasting distorting effect that skews the competitive edge against small businesses.

Third, federal support was perceived to be too little given the magnitude of the crisis. The PPP, for example, only supported between eight and 24 weeks of payroll costs, while average closure during the pandemic was significantly longer for a large percentage of businesses.

Access to financial assistance was also inversely correlated with size: 38 percent of microenterprises (with less than five employees) received no form of financial assistance during the pandemic, compared to 10 percent of businesses with 20 or more employees. Overall, none of the existing financial assistance programs are geared toward catalyzing green transformation in the private sector. Considering the significance of small businesses for economic and employment growth, social inclusion, and climate transition, there is a clear need for a cross-cutting policy initiative that promotes green recovery and long-term competitiveness among them.

Policy Recommendations

The best way to enable green recovery would be creating a Small Business Green Fund (SBGF) dedicated to financing climate transition among small businesses. Building on the experiences of the Paycheck Protection Program (PPP) and the Mainstreet Lending Program (MLP), the fund can be channeled through intermediary financial institutions in exchange for an operating fee that is paid by the government. Community Development Financial Institutions (CDFIs), Minority Depository Institutions, and other smaller, minority-oriented financial institutions could be prioritized to ensure fair representation of minorities, thus avoiding a repeat of the mistakes of the PPP and MLP programs that arguably benefited larger and better-connected businesses. The Fund will contribute towards a number of national policy priorities that form the centerpiece of President Biden's reform agenda, including racial equity and inclusion, the "made in all of America" program to revitalize American industries, and the commitment to achieve carbon neutrality by 2050 by bringing about "clean energy revolution and environmental justice."

Green projects that are eligible for funding are identified through standardized instruments for classifying sustainability performance, as explained in the next subsection. A decentralized, market-based approach for identifying, assessing, and verifying sustainability performance will be more effective in maximizing impact since policymakers may not necessarily know a priori the types of sustainable solutions that are most appropriate for climate transition among millions of businesses. To accommodate the diverse financial demands of small businesses, the fund is proposed to have components of green grants, green loans, and green bonds that differ in size, structure, interest rate, and maturity.

A Green Grants Fund will support sustainable investments and other expenditures by small businesses (with 50 workers or less) that have little or no recourse to external financing for their projects. Small grants of up to $100,000 can be used to fully cover small green investments by eligible businesses (such as solar panel fittings), while larger grants of up to $1,000,000 could be used to subsidize (by up to 50 percent) the investment cost of keystone green projects. Examples of such projects include research and development costs for producing marketable low-carbon technologies that can support climate transition. The fund is best administered by the Small Business Administration agency, which has experience in administering grants for small businesses. A portion of the fund can be dedicated to bolstering the capacity of the SBA to provide financial and technical support to facilitate climate transition.

A Green Loans Fund will provide small, affordable loans for financing projects that go beyond regulatory requirements and use the best available technology and/or the best environmental management practices. This fund will target small businesses employing 20 to 500 employees that need long-term finance for executing green projects. These loans can be structured based on the experiences of the Main Street Lending Program (MLP), which provided loans with a five-year maturity period, with deferral of principal payments for up to two years and deferral of interest payments for one year. As in MLP, lending financial institutions will take full responsibility for receiving applications and approving loans. The SBA (or the Treasury) participates in the program by purchasing a portion of the green loans, with the lending institution retaining the remaining share. To address different levels of financial need, the size of green loans could range between $100,000 and $50 million. Very small loans below $100,000 are best excluded to keep transaction costs low and to avoid increasing operating costs that could make the program expensive.

A Green Bonds Fund will finance green bond issuances by financial institutions that provide funding for green projects by small enterprises. It will also be used to provide (partial) guarantees and other credit enhancements for (nonfinancial) small business bond issuers to help them gain more favorable access to capital markets. Size restriction can be placed on the intermediary financial institutions to ensure that the fund does not go to institutions that are capable of independently issuing green bonds. To execute the Green Bonds Fund, the Treasury would have to partner with financial institutions that have experience in structuring and underwriting green bond issuances, such as such as the International Financial Corporation (IFC) or private banks. The partnering intermediaries can play an important role by providing technical assistance to the beneficiary financial institutions on the processes of bond issuance and subsequent distribution of proceeds.

Green bonds are innovative financial instruments that provide issuers with long-term loans conditional on green use of proceeds, which is tracked through impact reporting and external reviews. Although the market of green bonds is growing rapidly, it is dominated by sovereigns and large corporations, with an average issue size of $107 million in 2018. The large average size of green bonds could be due to the high transaction cost of issuing them, which limits the access of small businesses to the green bond market. The proposed fund will mitigate that by financing the purchase of green bonds issued by small and medium financial institutions that cater to small businesses. In addition, the fund can be used to provide credit enhancements in the form of partial guarantees to (nonfinancial) small businesses that face limited or costly access to securities markets. The green fund can also be used to complement private investment in green bond issuances by financing risky junior and mezzanine tranches, with the private sector financing less risky senior tranches. These risk mitigation measures can facilitate the maturity of the green bonds market by allowing small business issuers to build credit ratings, while also crowding in green investments by the private sector. To reduce transaction costs and attract institutional investors who have a preference for large issuances, the proposed fund can target green bonds with an issue size of up to $500 million.

Environmental Due Diligence

The green loans and green bonds schemes will be governed by detailed contractual agreements between the federal agencies administering the funds and financial intermediaries distributing them. The agreements will stipulate the beneficiaries of the funds, the specific environmental issues to be targeted, and procedures for interim monitoring and final evaluation of performance. It will also specify which external standards will be used for identifying projects that qualify for funding, and the measurement frameworks to be used for monitoring and evaluating performance. Climate financing in the European Union's recovery fund, for example, is guided by the sustainable finance taxonomy that provides a classification system for the sustainability impacts of various climate-related activities.

The agreements can also specify priority areas of economic activity that should be targeted by the financial intermediaries. Priority sectors or activities should be identified based on their emissions abatement potential; their contribution to green growth and jobs; their financial needs and; their ability to draw in private sector capital. Potential priority industries are those directly contributing to the development of climate technologies (e.g., innovators or producers of solar and hydrogen technologies) and industries with large carbon footprints (e.g., manufacturing, construction, agribusiness, transportation, and logistics, etc.).

Green projects that should be eligible or top priorities for funding can be identified through standardized instruments developed for this purpose. The EU's sustainable finance taxonomy, for example, defines sustainable economic activities as those making a substantive contribution to one of the following six environmental objectives: (1) climate change adaptation; (2) climate change mitigation; (3) protection of marine and water resources; (4) transition to circular economy; (5) pollution prevention and control and; (6) biodiversity protection. The taxonomy identifies sustainability screening criteria for 70 economic activities that have significant emissions footprints and hence need to be prioritized for climate change mitigation. The framework does not privilege specific economic activities as a priority for climate change adaptation, but provides sustainability screening criteria for a non-exhaustible list of 68 climate change adaptation activities.

There are a number of voluntary private sector standards for identifying projects that qualify for green financing. The Green Bond Principles (GBP) by the International Capital Market Association (ICMA) are widely used in the green bonds market to promote the transparency and integrity of disclosure and impact evaluation. The principles also provide a nonexclusive list of the types of project that can qualify for green bond financing including, inter alia, those contributing to improvements in renewable energy, energy efficiency, pollution control and prevention, resource conservation, sustainable land use, biodiversity preservation, climate change adaption, and eco-efficiency. The Science Based Targets Initiative (SBTi) helps small businesses with developing emissions reduction targets needed to meet the climate goals of the Paris Agreement, while also offering guidance on assessing and verifying performance. Lending institutions for the Small Business Green Recovery Fund can be required to adopt one or more third-party standards for identifying green projects.

Green loans and green bonds will require ex ante and ex post due diligence to ensure that the beneficiaries use the funds for the intended purpose. As the ultimate lender and investor, the SBA/the Treasury can demand a high degree of transparency on the use of proceeds, and the social and environmental impact of the investments. This could entail measurement, disclosure and verification of the environmental impact created through the use of proceeds using the best available standards. Typically, green bond issuers provide different types of external reviews to showcase the sustainable use of proceeds including audited verification, consultant review (e.g. second-party opinion), and certification against third-party standards (e.g. Climate Bond Standard). Although verification should ideally involve accredited, third-party auditors to confirm that performance and reporting follow agreed-upon standards, in practice less stringent verification mechanisms are used because of their costliness and complexity. The EU's upcoming legislation for Green Bond Standards is expected to address this limitation by proposing a centralized accreditation regime for auditors to enhance transparency, accountability, comparability, and credibility in the green bond market.

Conclusion

The proposed Small Business Green Recovery Fund aims to rejuvenate economic recovery while also catalyzing the transition to climate neutrality by 2050. The fund will incentivize small businesses to innovate and deploy green technologies, ensuring that climate transition gains momentum across the whole spectrum of businesses rather than remaining confined to large corporations. It will help reduce the growing performance gap between small businesses that were severely hit by the pandemic and larger enterprises that weathered the pandemic relatively well, and hence are more capable of making long-term green investments.

By facilitating climate transition in women- and minority-owned small businesses, it will also counteract income inequalities across businesses and communities that accelerated during the pandemic.

The proposed fund will advance multiple national goals and contribute to the Biden administration's plan for "building back better" toward an inclusive, climate-resilient, and globally competitive economy. The fund will draw in billions of dollars in additional private sector investment in green technologies, spawning the development and diffusion of innovations that will enable the U.S. to meet its obligations under the Paris Agreement. The fund will also spur the growth of the sustainable finance ecosystem by supporting the development, diversification, and deepening of the emerging green bonds market, thus promoting U.S. leadership in this strategic sector.

Footnotes

1. Only 20 percent of small businesses, however, hired additional workers, the remaining being self-employing sole proprietorships. The share of minority-owned small businesses that employ workers is estimated to be much smaller at 7.5 percent.
2. Kobe, K., & Schwinn, R. (2017). Small Business GDP 1998-2014. U.S. Small Business Administration Office of Advocacy. SBA Research paper.
3. OECD Structural and Demographic Business Statistics Database 2018. http://dx.doi.org/10.1787/sdbs-data-en Charts B, E. OECD Timely Indicators of Entrepreneurship Database 2018.
4. In late April 2020, 89.9 percent of small businesses reported experiencing a negative effect on operations due to COVID-19; this figure fell to 75 percent by mid-November.
5. Siemer, M. (2019). Employment effects of financial constraints during the Great Recession. *Review of Economics and Statistics*, 101(1), 16-29.
6. This is not counting some state-level green financing initiatives. California's Treasurer's Office, for example, has invested in World Bank Green Bonds, helping generate proceeds for funding sustainable projects.
7. In both the European Union and France, green strings were attached to government budgetary spending, but not on businesses receiving recovery support, to avoid cumbersome regulations that would hold back business recovery.

VIEWPOINT 4

> "In rebuilding after the crisis, sustainability is not an add-on. It's about building competitive advantage, lowering risk, getting ahead of new regulations, gaining ground with investors, and adjusting to new consumer demands."

Businesses Should Prioritize Sustainability Investments

Shalini Unnikrishnan, Chris Biggs, and Nidhi Singh

In the following viewpoint, Shalini Unnikrishnan, Chris Biggs, and Nidhi Singh argue that businesses should prioritize investments in sustainability, clean energy solutions, and resource efficiency—even when circumstances seem to call for short-term cost reductions. Both consumers and investors are increasingly aware of climate change and its associated risks and have demonstrated a growing desire to work with companies that are participating in the movement toward a greener, more sustainable economy. Moreover, the long-term savings that companies can expect from investments in efficiency and sustainability will help prepare them for future crises and downturns. Shalini Unnikrishnan is the global lead for societal impact in the Consumer and Social Impact practices at Boston Consulting Group (BCG). Chris Biggs is the managing director and senior partner at BCG's London-based Global Retail group. Nidhi Singh is a team manager for BCG's Consumer Products and Retail practice.

"Sustainability Matters Now More Than Ever for Consumer Companies," by Shalini Unnikrishnan, Chris Biggs, and Nidhi Singh, The Boston Consulting Group, August 11, 2020. Reprinted by permission. https://www.bcg.com/en-in/publications/2020/sustainability-matters-now-more-than-ever-for-consumer-companies

Is a Green Economy Beneficial to American Businesses and Investors?

As you read, consider the following questions:

1. According to the authors, how did the COVID-19 pandemic and the resulting economic crisis affect consumer attitudes toward sustainability and other green values?
2. What are some of the reasons why the authors emphasize the importance of adopting a long-term perspective when it comes to investments in sustainability?
3. What are some of the risks that companies may face if they elect to postpone investing in sustainable solutions?

When a global pandemic is disrupting your supply chain and you're scrambling to get products in bags and on shelves while ensuring that manufacturing plants operate safely, focusing on reducing single-use plastics or cutting water consumption might seem a stretch. But what if failing to address these things ends up costing money and weakening the business down the line?

This is what we are hearing when we talk to the heads of the leading consumer companies. They know that consumer and investor pressure to embrace sustainability is not going away. They know that abandoning their efforts now could pose serious risks to the business in the future and make picking up the sustainability agenda later impractical or unaffordable. And they are looking for pragmatic ways in which to advance their goals.

It is true that some environmental regulations have been eased because of the pandemic. Prompted by health concerns, for example, some regulators have reversed bans on single-use plastics.

But as governments plan the relaunching of their economies, they are thinking about how to recover to a fair, resource-efficient, and resilient society. For example, a quarter of the European Union's €750 billion ($868 billion) COVID-19 recovery fund has been earmarked for climate action. The fund also excludes environmentally damaging investments. And in South Korea, the newly elected government is pursuing a Green New Deal that includes a carbon tax, a focus on renewable energy investments, an obligation to end coal investments, and a hydrogen strategy.

Among consumers, the crisis has driven the sustainability agenda forward. Consumers already wanted to know more about the origins of what they buy. Now, they are more focused than ever on health and safety and are showing strong support for the businesses in their local communities.

A recent BCG survey examined how the pandemic has shifted global consumer attitudes toward environmental issues. Ninety percent of consumer respondents said they were equally or more concerned about these issues after the COVID-19 outbreak, and nearly 95% said they believed their personal actions could help reduce unsustainable waste, tackle climate change, and protect wildlife and biodiversity, with 27% to 30% noting that this belief had strengthened as a result of the crisis.

Meanwhile, online retail has taken on new significance in people's lives during the pandemic. And with this trend expected to last beyond the crisis, companies face increasing pressure to compete in the digital sphere.

Savvy consumer companies have been responding. Our analysis shows that, on the basis of their actions, they fall into three broad categories:

- At a minimum, companies have been implementing programs focused on employee welfare, introducing social distancing and hygiene practices, and support for suppliers.
- Some companies are doing more by adapting sustainability agendas to the shifts in consumer demand prompted by the pandemic, such as localizing supply chains, introducing technologies such as blockchain to enhance transparency on product sourcing and manufacturing, adapting pack types and sizes for online sales, and prioritizing products suitable for consumption at home.
- Really savvy consumer companies are doing things differently. These companies are seeking new opportunities by integrating sustainability across core business operations and making it

part of the organization's strategic fabric, whether through minimizing packaging, cutting waste in supply chains, or optimizing delivery routes.

Given that companies are already making such fundamental shifts in their strategies, product lines, and operational models, it makes sense to build in sustainability along the way—rather than trying to retrofit at a later stage.

There is another compelling reason for maintaining a focus on sustainability efforts: Competitors are moving forward aggressively on their agendas.

When it comes to traceability, for example, Unilever has added to its sustainability goals—net zero emissions from its products, from cradle to shelf, by 2039 and investments of €1 billion ($1.1 billion) in climate-friendly initiatives over the next decade—with a plan to label all its 70,000 products with information on how much greenhouse gas they generated through raw ingredients, manufacturing, and shipping, right up to the point the product is picked up off the shelf.

In April, P&G announced that Old Spice and Secret deodorants would appear in plastic-free, paper packaging in certain Walmart stores as part of a 2030 goal to reach 100% recyclable or reusable packaging and a 50% reduction in virgin petroleum plastic consumption.

And in May, Mondelez announced it was on track to reach its targets of 100% recyclable packaging and 100% sustainable cocoa sourcing for chocolate by 2025. Nestlé is also making progress on its commitment to make 100% of its packaging recyclable or reusable by 2025, and it plans to reduce by one-third its use of virgin plastics by that year.

Evidence shows that investors may reward companies for these approaches as part of a broader focus on ESG (environmental, social, and governance) factors—particularly since ESG funds have outperformed benchmarks during the market downturn. In fact, BCG's Investor Pulse Check found that 51% of investors think it's important for healthy companies to pursue their ESG priorities fully as they navigate the crisis, even if it means lower earnings per share.

This means that putting a pause on sustainability agendas is a risky move. The difference between companies that scale back and those that move forward on sustainability will be that, in a postpandemic world, the latter will be in a better position to mitigate regulatory risks and benefit from consumer and investor preferences.

Of course, none of this is easy. And even before the crisis, many companies' sustainability goals were looking hard to hit. However, this is not a reason for giving up. Moreover, the choice is not between launching a radically accelerated sustainability strategy and doing nothing. There is a third way.

Companies should focus on building back, but while doing so they need to ensure they're building back better, reconsidering supply chain practices and implementing digital strategies that also advance transparency, traceability, and impact measurement. They should include the sustainability team in discussions about how to embed environmental and social impact into the changes being made as part of the recovery strategy.

Given the new challenges, current sustainability strategies need to be refreshed. To help with this, we've laid out a ten-point checklist for embedding societal impact into business strategy.

Different countries are at different stages. Some are still battling infections. Some are flattening the curve. Others are reopening their economies. And resurgences of infection may accompany resumption of normal life. Companies must learn to live in a state where they are not necessarily in panic mode but are constantly ready to fight small fires. Of course, they also need to focus on building back. But sustainability should be considered a core part of that.

This means elevating the significance of sustainability across the enterprise by creating chief sustainability officer positions (similar to such positions as chief digital officer). Early examples appeared in 2004, when DuPont and Nike made CSO appointments. Today, a growing number of companies—among them Diageo, P&G, Mastercard, Nissan, Ralph Lauren, and Tyson Foods—are making their first CSO appointments.

In rebuilding after the crisis, sustainability is not an add-on. It's about building competitive advantage, lowering risk, getting ahead of new regulations, gaining ground with investors, and adjusting to new consumer demands. And companies can get a better return on investment from the operational and supply chain changes that are already being made by embedding sustainability within those changes. A sustainability focus also builds resilience—although the link between sustainability and resilience was already evident, it has become even clearer during the pandemic.

For companies, all this flows back into long-term success. As we look into the future, one thing is clear: While some will cede ground on sustainability and social impact, consumer companies that choose to reset and reengage will make rapid progress on their goals—and that will not only enable them to reap greater benefit from their recovery investments but also give them a distinct competitive advantage.

VIEWPOINT 5

> *"Few consumers who report positive attitudes toward eco-friendly products and services follow through with their wallets."*

Relying on Green Consumers Can Be Risky and Challenging

Katherine White, David J. Hardisty, and Rishad Habib

In the following viewpoint, Katherine White, David J. Hardisty, and Rishad Habib argue that despite the growing awareness of environmental issues among consumers and the bourgeoning sustainable consumption movement, the market for green products can be risky and unpredictable. Many consumers have negative associations with eco-friendly products and even those who express a desire to purchases sustainable products often prioritize cost and convenience over other factors when their money is on the line. The authors propose a number of strategies that businesses can implement to help manage these challenges while acknowledging that the green consumer market is likely to remain somewhat vexing in the near-term. Katherine White is senior associate dean of the Marketing and Behavioral Science Division at UBC Sauder School of Business. David J. Hardisty is chair of the Marketing and Behavioral Science Division at UBC Sauder School of Business. Rishad Habib is associate professor in marketing at Ryerson University.

"The Elusive Green Consumer," by Katherine White, David J. Hardisty, and Rishad Habib, *Harvard Business Review*, July-August 2019. Reprinted by permission.

Is a Green Economy Beneficial to American Businesses and Investors?

As you read, consider the following questions:

1. What do the authors mean when they refer to the "intention-action gap" in the green consumer market?
2. What are some of the negative associations that consumers exhibit toward green and eco-friendly products?
3. How do social norms affect consumer attitudes toward green and eco-friendly products?

On the surface, there has seemingly never been a better time to launch a sustainable offering. Consumers—particularly Millennials—increasingly say they want brands that embrace purpose and sustainability. Indeed, one recent report revealed that certain categories of products with sustainability claims showed twice the growth of their traditional counterparts. Yet a frustrating paradox remains at the heart of green business: Few consumers who report positive attitudes toward eco-friendly products and services follow through with their wallets. In one recent survey 65% said they want to buy purpose-driven brands that advocate sustainability, yet only about 26% actually do so.

Narrowing this "intention-action gap" is important not just for meeting corporate sustainability goals but also for the planet. Unilever estimates that almost 70% of its greenhouse gas footprint depends on which products customers choose and whether they use and dispose of them in a sustainable manner—for example, by conserving water and energy while doing the laundry or recycling containers properly after use.

We have been studying how to encourage sustainable consumption for several years, performing our own experiments and reviewing research in marketing, economics, and psychology. The good news is that academics have learned a lot about how to align consumers' behaviors with their stated preferences. Much of the research has focused on public interventions by policy makers—but the findings can be harnessed by any organization that wishes to nudge consumers toward sustainable purchasing and behavior. Synthesizing these insights, we have identified five actions for companies to consider: use social influence, shape good habits, leverage the domino effect, decide whether to talk to the heart or the brain, and favor experiences over ownership.

Use Social Influence

In 2010 the city of Calgary, Alberta, had a problem. It had recently rolled out a program called grasscycling, which involves residents' leaving grass clippings to naturally decompose on a lawn after mowing, rather than bagging them to be taken to a landfill. The city had created an informational campaign about the program that highlighted its benefits: Grasscycling would return valuable nutrients to the soil, protect the lawn, and help the soil retain moisture. What's more, this sustainable behavior actually required less work from the individual. But initial adoption rates were lower than the city had expected.

One of us (White) advised Calgary to try to change residents' behavior using "social norms"—informal understandings within a social group about what constitutes acceptable behavior. Scores of studies have shown that humans have a strong desire to fit in and will conform to the behavior of those around them. To leverage this motivation, White and her colleague Bonnie Simpson worked with the city on a large-scale field study in which messages were left on residents' doors: "Your neighbors are grasscycling. You can too" and "Most people are finding ways to reduce the materials that are going to the landfill—you can contribute by grasscycling." Within two weeks this simple intervention resulted in almost twice as much residential grasscycling as did the control condition.

Harnessing the power of social influence is one of the most effective ways to elicit pro-environmental behaviors in consumption as well. Telling online shoppers that other people were buying eco-friendly products led to a 65% increase in making at least one sustainable purchase. Telling buffet diners that the norm was to not take too much at once (and that it was OK to return for seconds)

The High Cost of Green Goods

For consumers wanting to buy "green," the choices these days appear endless. Unless, that is, you're on a budget.

Eco-friendly straws, sneakers, garments and packaging are often pricier than their conventional counterparts, leaving poor and middle-class people with not much of a choice, according to Bloomberg.

"There's a lot of innovation going on with sustainability right now, it's just not really affordable," Alexis Benveniste, who recently wrote about the phenomenon for Bloomberg, told CBS News. "It's hard to scale when you're paying more for a green product."

For some products, such as organic food, the higher sticker price is reflective of the higher cost of creating that type of food. But others charge more simply because they can. "Eco-friendly" or "sustainable" branding is increasingly used as a marketing strategy to distinguish products as premium or elite, making them almost certain to appeal to wealthier shoppers.

Benveniste wrote, "It's no coincidence that it costs $20 to use reusable beeswax instead of plastic wrap to keep your food fresh, and you can even buy shoes that are completely made from recycled plastic—but they'll cost you $145 a pair."

Since the U.S. economy does not regularly impose a price on pollution, shopping in a "green" way is still a matter of consumer (or corporate) choice. That spells trouble in the long term, even in a world where most people are environmentally conscious. Shoppers do care about the environment, polls show—until they're forced to make a trade-off.

"[W[hen consumers are forced to make trade-offs between product attributes or helping the environment, the environment almost never wins," the MIT Sloan Management Review found recently.

That's why, for some companies, "green" marketing is more of a signaling strategy than anything else. Consider widespread plastic straw bans. This tactic, which Benveniste calls "a conversation piece," addresses just a fraction of one percent of the plastic waste humans dump into the planet each year.

If companies really wanted to make a dent in sustainability, "you'd think they would start with takeout containers, or other, bigger things," she said. "Straws are easier to scale…and they're not really a necessity."

"Buying 'Green' Is Too Pricey for the Average Consumer," by Irina Ivanova, CBS News, March 12, 2019.

decreased food waste by 20.5%. A major predictor of whether people will install solar panels is whether their close-by neighbors have done so. And, in perhaps the most dramatic finding, telling university students that other commuters were ditching their cars in favor of more-sustainable modes of transportation (such as cycling) led them to use sustainable transport five times as often as did those who were simply given information about alternatives.

Sometimes social motivators can backfire, however. If only a few people are engaging in a sustainable behavior, it may appear to be not socially approved of, thus discouraging adoption. In such instances companies can enlist advocates to promote the positive elements of the product or action. Advocates are most compelling when they themselves have undertaken the behavior. One study found that when an advocate related why he or she had installed residential solar panels, 63% more people followed suit than when the advocate had not actually installed panels.

Social norms may also turn off certain consumer segments. For example, some men associate sustainability with femininity, leading them to avoid sustainable options. But if a brand is already strongly associated with masculinity, this effect can be mitigated. Jack Daniel's, for example, embeds sustainability in many aspects of its business. Taglines such as "With all due respect to progress, the world could use a little less plastic" (accompanied by a row of wooden barrels) and "Even Jack Daniel's waste is too good to waste" link sustainability to quality and great taste. Because the company sells waste products and unused resources to other industries, it sends zero waste to landfills. And whiskey fans can buy used charcoal from the mellowing vats in the form of barbecue briquettes for grilling at home, reaffirming traditional masculine values. All this highlights the company's support for the work ethic, the land and the air, and the community in which Jack Daniel's operates. To avoid losing its standing as a rugged, masculine brand, it has expertly integrated sustainability into its existing branding.

In another example, people who lean right on the political spectrum are sometimes less open to engaging in eco-friendly behaviors because they associate them with a liberal political ideology. In the United States, for example, Republicans were less likely to buy a compact fluorescent light bulb that they knew was more energy-efficient than an incandescent bulb when it was labeled "Protect the Environment" than when that label was missing.

A solution is to make communications resonate with Republicans' political identity—for example, by referencing duty, authority, and consistency with in-group norms. In one field study Republican residents recycled more after being told, "You can join the fight by recycling with those like you in your community. Your actions help us to do our civic duty because recycling is the responsible thing to do in our society. Because of people like you, we can follow the advice of important leaders by recycling. You CAN join the fight!" That appeal didn't resonate in the same way with Democrats, who were more likely to respond to messaging around social welfare. Another solution is to focus on values that everyone shares, such as family, community, prosperity, and security.

Consumers often have negative associations with sustainable product options, viewing them as being of lower quality, less aesthetically pleasing, and more expensive. In one example, when people valued strength in a product—a car cleaner, say—they were less likely to choose sustainable options. One way to offset such negative associations is to highlight the product's positively viewed attributes—such as innovativeness, novelty, and safety. For example, Tesla focuses on the innovative design and functional performance of its cars more than on their green credentials—a message that resonates with its target market. This also helps overcome the concern of some men that green products are feminine.

Social influence can be turbocharged in three ways. The first is by simply making sustainable behaviors more evident to others. In some of Katherine White's research, people were asked to choose between an eco-friendly granola bar (which had the tagline "Good for you and the environment") and a traditional granola bar ("A healthy, tasty snack"). The sustainable option was twice as likely to be chosen when others were present than when the choice was made in private. Other researchers have found similar effects with products ranging from eco-friendly hand sanitizers to high-efficiency automobiles. The city of Halifax, Nova Scotia, found that when residents were required to put their household waste in clear bags, thus making the contents of their trash (which often included items that should have been recycled or composted) visible to the neighbors, the amount of garbage that went to the landfill decreased by 31%.

A second way to increase the impact of social influence is to make people's commitments to eco-friendly behavior public. For example, asking hotel guests to signal that they agree to reuse towels by hanging a card on their room door increased towel reuse by 20% In a similar study, asking hotel guests to wear a pin symbolizing their commitment to participating in an energy-conservation program increased towel reuse by 40%. And a study aimed at reducing vehicle idle time when children were being picked up at school asked some parents to display a window sticker reading "For Our Air: I Turn My Engine Off When Parked." The intervention resulted in a 73% decrease in idling time.

A third approach is to use healthy competition between social groups. In one example, communicating that another group of students was behaving in a positively viewed way ("We are trying to encourage students to compost…. Recently, a survey… found that Computing Science students are the most effective in composting efforts when compared across the student groups") made business students more than twice as likely to compost their biodegradable coffee cups. When the World Wildlife Fund and its partner volunteer organizations wanted to raise awareness about sustainable actions for Earth Hour, a global lights-off event, they spearheaded friendly energy-saving competitions between cities. The program has spread through social diffusion: It began in Sydney, Australia, in 2007 and now reaches 188 countries, with 3.5 billion social media mentions from January to March of

2018 and lights switched off at almost 18,000 landmarks during Earth Hour 2018.

Shape Good Habits

Humans are creatures of habit. Many behaviors, such as how we commute to work, what we buy, what we eat, and how we dispose of products and packaging, are part of our regular routines. Often the key to spreading sustainable consumer behaviors is to first break bad habits and then encourage good ones.

Habits are triggered by cues found in familiar contexts. For example, using disposable coffee cups (a habit repeated a staggering 500 billion times a year across the globe) may be a response to cues, such as the default cup provided by the barista and a trash bin illustrated with a picture of a cup, both common in coffee shops.

Companies can use design features to eliminate negative habits and substitute positive ones. The simplest and probably most effective approach is to make sustainable behavior the default option. For example, researchers in Germany discovered that when green electricity was set as the default option in residential buildings, 94% of individuals stuck with it. In other cases, making green options—such as reusing towels or receiving electronic rather than paper bank statements—the default increased uptake of the more sustainable option. In full-service restaurants in California, drinks no longer come with plastic straws; customers must explicitly request one. Another strategy is to make the desired action easier—by, for example, placing recycling bins nearby, requiring less complex sorting of recyclables, or providing free travel cards for public transport.

Three subtle techniques can help shape positive habits: using prompts, providing feedback, and offering incentives.

Prompts might be text messages reminding people to engage in desired behaviors, such as cycling, jogging, or commuting in some other eco-friendly way to work. Prompts work best when they are easy to understand and received where the behavior will take place, and when people are motivated to engage in the behavior.

In one study just placing prompts near recycling bins increased recycling by 54%.

Feedback sometimes tells people how they performed alone and sometimes compares their performance to that of others. Household energy bills that show how consumers' usage compares with that of neighbors can encourage energy saving. If the behavior is repeatedly performed—driving a car in varying traffic conditions, for example—real-time feedback like what the Toyota Prius offers drivers about their gas mileage can be effective.

Incentives can take any number of forms. In the UK, Coca-Cola has partnered with Merlin Entertainments to offer "reverse vending machines" from which consumers receive half-price entry tickets to theme parks when they recycle their plastic drink bottles. Incentives should be used with care, because if they are removed, the desired behavior may disappear too. Another concern is that they may undermine consumers' intrinsic desire to adopt a behavior. In a study in the *Journal of Consumer Psychology*, "Are Two Reasons Better Than One?," researchers found that combining external incentives ("Save money!") with intrinsic motives ("Save the environment!") resulted in less preference for a sustainable product than did intrinsic appeals alone. The authors hypothesized that this occurred because an external motivation can "crowd out" an intrinsic desire.

Even using these tactics, it is almost always difficult to break habits. But major life changes—such as moving to a new neighborhood, starting a new job, or acquiring a new group of friends—may create an exception, because such changes make people more likely to consciously evaluate and experiment with their routines. One study examined 800 households, half of which had recently moved. Half the participants in each group (half the movers and half the nonmovers) were given an intervention consisting of an interview, a selection of eco-friendly items, and information about sustainability. The movers were significantly more likely than the nonmovers to engage in environmentally friendly behaviors after the intervention.

Leverage the Domino Effect

One of the benefits of encouraging consumers to form desirable habits is that it can create positive spillover: People like to be consistent, so if they adopt one sustainable behavior, they are often apt to make other positive changes in the future. After IKEA launched a sustainability initiative called Live Lagom (lagom means "the right amount" in Swedish), it studied the sustainability journey in depth among a core group of its customers. The company found that although people may begin with a single step—such as reducing household food waste—they often move on to act in other domains, such as energy conservation. IKEA observed a snowball effect as well: People would begin with small actions and build to more meaningful ones. For example, buying LED light bulbs might lead to wearing warmer clothing and turning down the thermostat, changing curtains and blinds to decrease heat loss, insulating doors and windows, buying energy-efficient appliances, installing a programmable thermostat, and so on.

It is important to remember that negative spillover can occur too: A sustainable action may lead someone to subsequently behave less sustainably. Termed licensing by researchers, this occurs when a consumer feels that an initial ethical action confers permission to behave less virtuously in the future. In one example, researchers found that people who had performed a virtual green shopping task were less likely to behave prosocially (in a game they were less likely to help others by allocating resources) than those who had performed a virtual conventional shopping task. In other examples, people use more paper when they can show that they are recycling and use more of a product (such as mouthwash, glass cleaner, or hand sanitizer) when it is a sustainable one. Similarly, car models with increased fuel efficiency may lead people to drive more miles, and more-efficient home heating and cooling systems may lead them to increase usage.

Hope and pride can be particularly useful in driving sustainable consumption.

Companies can take steps to lessen the risk of negative spillover. They can ensure that the first sustainable action is particularly effortful, which seems to build commitment. When consumers are asked to make smaller commitments, it is best not to publicize those actions, because that may lead to something researchers call slacktivism. In one study, participants who had engaged in token support for a cause that demonstrated to others that they were "good people"—such as joining a "public" Facebook group or signing an online petition—were less likely to engage in a private task later, such as volunteering for the cause. However, those who privately joined a Facebook group or signed a petition were more likely to see the cause as reflecting their true values and to follow through. Note that this differs from the earlier example of giving pins to hotel guests who choose energy-efficient options, because in that study wearing a pin was explicitly tied to a commitment to perform a sustainable action. Someone who sees a token initial behavior as engagement in a cause often performs fewer positive actions in the future.

Decide Whether to Talk to the Heart or the Brain

How companies communicate with consumers has an enormous influence on the adoption of sustainable behaviors. When getting ready to launch or promote a product or a campaign, marketers often have a choice between emotional levers and rational arguments. Either can be effective—but only if certain conditions are met.

The Emotional Appeal

People are more likely to engage in a behavior when they derive positive feelings from doing so. This core precept is often overlooked when it comes to sustainability, for which ad campaigns are likely to emphasize disturbing warnings. Research has found that hope and pride are particularly useful in driving sustainable consumption. Bacardi and Lonely Whale cultivate hope in their collaboration to eliminate one billion single-use plastic straws, and they use the hashtag #thefuturedoesntsuck to promote events and call for consumer action. And when people in one study were publicly praised each week for their energy-efficiency efforts, thus engendering pride, they saved more energy than a group that was given small (up to €5) weekly financial rewards.

Guilt is a more complicated emotional tool. Research by White and colleagues suggests that it can be an effective motivator but should be used carefully. In one experiment, when accountability was subtly highlighted (participants were asked to make a product choice in a public setting), consumers reported anticipating future guilt if they failed to shop for green products, and 84% chose fair trade options. However, when an explicit guilt appeal was used ("How can you enjoy a cup of tea knowing that the people who produce it are not being treated fairly?"), they became angry, upset, or irritable, and only 40% chose the fair trade option. Indeed, an abundance of other research confirms that activating moderate amounts of guilt, sadness, or fear, is more effective than trying to elicit a strong reaction. This research suggests that charity or cause appeals that use particularly emotive images (such as explicit images of suffering children) may not be as effective as less heavy-handed ones.

The Rational Appeal

In 2010 Unilever launched a campaign to draw attention to the fact that although some palm oil harvesting leads to rain forest destruction, its palm oil is all sustainably farmed. Printed on a photo of a rain forest was the tagline "What you buy at the supermarket can change the world.... Small actions, big difference." The company was leveraging decades-old research findings that people are unlikely to undertake a behavior unless they have a sense of what researchers call self-efficacy—confidence that their actions will have a meaningful impact. Thus one key to marketing a sustainable product is communicating what effect its use will have on the environment.

Although information about sustainable behaviors and their outcomes can be persuasive, how the information is framed is critical, especially for products with high up-front costs and delayed benefits. Recent research by one of us (Hardisty) found that consumers who are buying appliances or electronics typically don't think about energy efficiency—and even if they do, they don't care as much about future energy saving as about the up-front price. However, in a field study at a chain of drugstores, labeling the "10-year dollar cost" of energy for each product increased energy-efficient purchases from 12% to 48%. Such labels are effective for three reasons: They make the future consequences more salient, they frame the information in dollars (which consumers care about) rather than energy saving (which they often don't), and they scale up energy costs tenfold.

Indeed, people's tendency to prefer avoiding losses over making equivalent gains—what psychologists call loss aversion—can help marketers frame choices by communicating what's at stake. For instance, photos showing how glaciers have receded can be a powerful means of conveying environmental losses associated with climate change. White and her colleagues Rhiannon MacDonnell and Darren Dahl found that in the context of residential recycling, a loss-framed message ("Think about what will be lost in our community if we don't keep recycling") works best when it's combined with specific details about the behavior, such as when to put out the recycling cart, what materials are recyclable, and so forth. That's because people in a loss-framed mindset tend to want concrete ways to deal with a problem.

In addition, messages that focus on local impacts and local reference points are particularly powerful. That's why New York City's recent waste-reduction advertising campaign illustrated that all the garbage thrown out in the city on one day could fill the Empire State Building. Messages that communicate the concrete effects of sustainable consumer behavior change in other ways can also be effective. Tide encourages consumers to take the #CleanPledge and wash their clothes in cold water. Not only is this a consumer commitment, but the campaign communicates clear consequences, such as "Switching to cold water for one year can save enough energy to charge your phone for a lifetime." Another tactic is giving consumers something tangible to display their support of a brand or a cause and reporting clear outcomes. For example, 4ocean lets consumers know that for every upcycled bracelet they buy from the company, one pound of trash will be removed from the ocean.

Favor Experiences Over Ownership

Along with working to change consumer behavior, some companies have found success with business models that seemingly make consumers more open to green alternatives. In the "experience economy," companies offer experiential options as an alternative to material goods. For example, Honeyfund allows wedding gift givers to bypass cookie-cutter registries filled with typical household goods and instead contribute to destination honeymoons, gourmet dinners, and other adventures for the bride and groom. Tinggly, whose tagline is "Give stories, not stuff," also lets consumers buy adventures rather than tangible products as gifts. In addition to the potential sustainability benefit, research shows, giving an experience makes both giver and receiver happier, leads to stronger personal connections, and cultivates more-positive memories.

The sharing economy is enjoying similar success. Indeed, some of the leading growth models in recent years have involved businesses that neither develop nor sell new products or services but instead facilitate access to existing ones—which often means a much smaller environmental footprint. Businesses have sprung up to offer sharing and borrowing for everything from clothing and accessories (Rent the Runway and Bag Borrow or Steal) to vehicles (Zipcar and car2go), vacation rentals (Airbnb), and even on-demand tractors in Africa (Hello Tractor). However, sharing services can lead consumers to choose the easy-to-access option (such as an Uber or Lyft ride) rather than a more sustainable one, such as walking, biking, or taking public transport. Thus it's worth carefully considering what impact the service a company offers will have on consumers' ultimate behavior. Lyft has responded to this concern by committing to offset its operations globally, "through the direct funding of emission mitigation efforts, including the reduction of emissions in the automotive manufacturing process, renewable energy programs, forestry projects, and the capture of emissions from landfills," resulting in carbon-neutral rides for all.

Other companies have won customers over by offering to recycle products after use. Both Eileen Fisher and Patagonia encourage customers to buy high-quality pieces of their clothing, wear them as long as possible, and then return them to the company to be refurbished and resold. Thus one way to encourage eco-friendly consumer behavior is to build elements of sustainability into how products are used and ultimately disposed of.

Making Sustainability Resonate

Despite the growing momentum behind sustainable business practices, companies still strive to communicate their brands' sustainability to consumers in ways that heighten brand relevance, increase market share, and fuel a shift toward a culture of sustainable living. We have offered a menu of tools—informed by behavioral science—that can help. We recommend that companies work to understand the wants and needs of their target market, along with the barriers and benefits to realizing behavioral change, and tailor their strategies accordingly. We also recommend pilot A/B testing to determine which tactics work best.

Using marketing fundamentals to connect consumers with a brand's purpose, showing benefits over and above conventional options, and making sustainability irresistible are central challenges for businesses in the coming decades. As more and more succeed, sustainable business will become smart business.

VIEWPOINT 6

> "If companies making positive inroads on climate protection flourish, then the communities where those companies are working have a real chance to thrive."

The Business Community Can Help Manage the Transition to a Cleaner, More Efficient Economy

Sanya Carley and David Konisky

In the following viewpoint, Sanya Carley and David Konisky discuss how the business community can play a leadership role and help to manage the various costs of the United States' transition toward a cleaner, more sustainable economic system. They emphasize the importance of paying attention to vulnerable communities, including areas like Appalachia and rural Texas, where the economy depends largely on fossil fuel–based activities. They also highlight emerging business models, like subscription-based community solar programs and energy service companies (ESCOs) that have used innovative strategies to expand into underserved areas. Sanya Carley is associate professor and chair of the Policy Analysis and Public Finance Department at Indiana University. David M. Konisky is associate professor in the School of Public and Environmental Affairs at Indiana University.

"What Would the Green New Deal Mean for Businesses?" by Sanya Carley and David Konisky, *Harvard Business Review*, February 28, 2019. Reprinted by permission.

America's Infrastructure and the Green Economy

As you read, consider the following questions:

1. Why will the transition toward a cleaner economy prove more difficult and costly for certain regions?
2. What kinds of business opportunities do the authors suggest may be available as part of the effort to reclaim abandoned coal mines?
3. What do the authors mean when they refer to the "split incentive problem" with respect to renters and landlords?

This month, Democrats in the U.S. Congress, led by newly elected representative Alexandria Ocasio-Cortez, introduced a resolution calling for a Green New Deal. This nonbinding resolution is a wide-ranging and ambitious call for government-led efforts to address the causes of climate change, to invest in programs that will help communities fight its detrimental effects, and to do so in a way that is inclusive, equitable, and just.

To successfully implement the climate change mitigation goals of the Green New Deal—which include ultimately achieving net-zero greenhouse gas emissions—the United States would need to deploy cleaner energy technologies, invest in energy innovation, and eventually convert the transportation sector to an electric mode of operation. These changes would help displace incumbent fossil fuels—coal in the near term, and oil and natural gas in the decades that follow.

In our opinion, given the urgency of climate change, and the disproportionate role that the United States has contributed to the problem, the goals of the Green New Deal are laudable. There is, however, a cost to such a transition. In our research over the past several years, we have analyzed ways in which the energy transition can produce adverse consequences, and worked to identify which communities are most vulnerable, and why. We have found that moving toward cleaner energy sources will continue to disproportionately affect communities whose economies and public finances rely on the extraction and use of fossil fuels. In Appalachia and other coal-mining regions, a further decline in production will lead to additional job losses, tax revenue erosion, and otherwise weakened socioeconomic conditions. Communities hosting coal-fired power plant operations may be similarly affected. A transition to cleaner sources of energy may also result in increased prices to power homes and transportation, which will place further financial burdens on households that spend a higher share of their income on energy. Finally, some communities will be excluded from the benefits of clean energy jobs due to a mismatch of skills and a lack of training opportunities, as well as access to new, efficient, and low-carbon energy technologies due to a lack of affordability or access.

These vulnerabilities are implicit to the goals of the Green New Deal, and its proponents envision that the government will take the lead role in both hastening the transition and ensuring that traditionally marginalized communities reap the benefits. The government has a key role to play, but so does the private sector. Companies can work to make technologies more broadly available, develop inclusive business models, and target hard-hit locations. Taking advantage of these early opportunities will not only help transform and protect vulnerable communities, it will also allow companies to secure new modes of revenue.

We suggest two broad and complementary opportunities for businesses:

Support Green Initiatives

Companies can help reduce the burdens of the energy transition by supporting economically sustainable low-carbon initiatives. Former and declining coal mining regions are on the economic frontlines of the transition. Many such regions in Appalachia and elsewhere are suffering job losses and disruption to the economic and social fabric of their communities. Economic development opportunities targeted to these areas, as well as those that are likely to be affected in the years to come, can help revive stagnating local economies and insulate them from the downsides of the transition.

One approach is to create new economic enterprises where coal extraction previously thrived. The Rocky Mountain Institute recently released a report as a part of its Sunshine for Mines initiative that evaluates second-life opportunities for abandoned coal mines, and provides businesses with an assessment tool to help them calculate the net present value of alternative uses. Possible second-life opportunities highlighted in this initiative include using the abandoned mine to house alternative energy sources such as pumped hydroelectricity or solar panels. The Reclaiming Appalachia Coalition is also working to help identify feasible opportunities for coal mine reclamation. Among them are several agricultural ventures such as CBD and hemp farms, a lavender field land conversion, outdoor recreation resorts, and recycling and reuse centers.

In other areas, businesses can be more proactive in their efforts to expand access to renewable energy. By working directly with local governments, companies can aid disadvantaged populations through urban neighborhood energy deployment efforts. In 2016, DTE Energy took this approach and partnered with the City of Detroit to install over 6,500 solar panels at O'Shea Park on Detroit's west side, providing energy to over 450 Detroit households. Such developments provide all residents, not just those with the highest incomes, the opportunity to access clean, carbon-free energy.

Develop Inclusive Business Models

Two new energy business models have evolved over the past decade that demonstrate possibilities for specifically targeting vulnerable populations: subscription-based community solar and energy service companies (ESCOs). In subscription-based community solar, people buy a subscription to a solar project that is owned and operated by a utility, another energy provider, or their community. They reap the benefits of solar access—reduced emissions and possibly financial savings—without incurring the large up-front cost that comes with purchasing and installing their own solar panels. In ESCOs, firms help other companies design a plan for energy savings through energy efficiency, conservation, or by installing new renewable energy technologies on-site. The ESCO is paid through a portion of the energy cost savings.

New business models for utilities are also important. Utilities can serve functions such as running community solar programs and providing energy efficiency services. They can also provide direct consumer load controls, rent storage systems for residential applications, and other consumer-oriented energy services that help extend the benefits of the energy transition to all communities, not just those that are wealthy.

These relatively new business models help individuals and organizations overcome the challenge of making large up-front investments in efficient technologies, but they are not perfect. Additional innovation will be needed to ensure that the clean energy transition is actually inclusive. Low-to-moderate income households that are more likely to invest in community solar programs, for example, often have poor credit profiles that limit their opportunities for participation. Reaching these populations will therefore require energy providers to devise creative financing options. In the case of ESCOs, members of under-represented groups disproportionately live in older, less energy efficient housing with significant opportunities for energy costs savings. Given the large proportion of renters, ESCOs will need to devise programs targeted at landlords to overcome the widely recognized split incentive problem.

Of course, companies cannot be expected to act alone, or pursue business models that are not profitable. Federal, state, and local government need to do their part to create incentives, or at least not put up barriers, to facilitate the inclusivity of the energy transition. Government also needs to create new programs that encourage companies to partner more directly with public and nonprofit organizations to develop strategies for expanding access to efficiency programs and renewable energy to households with limited financial means.

If companies making positive inroads on climate protection flourish, then the communities where those companies are working have a real chance to thrive. The Green New Deal has amplified the importance of inclusion and equity in the already intense debate about the best ways to accelerate the energy transition in the United States. Given the urgency and magnitude of the climate problem, we need all hands on deck.

Periodical and Internet Sources Bibliography

The following articles have been selected to supplement the diverse views presented in this chapter.

Alicia Adamczyk, "Why 'Greenwashing' Is an Issue for Sustainable Investments—and How to Avoid It," CNBC, April 23, 2021, https://www.cnbc.com/2021/04/23/what-to-know-about-greenwashing-in-sustainable-investments.html.

Abha Bhattarai, "Online Shopping Is Booming. Start-Ups Have a Few Ideas to Make It More Sustainable," *Washington Post*, February 17, 2021, https://www.washingtonpost.com/business/2021/02/17/online-shopping-sustainable-reusable-box-delivery.

Trang Chu Minh, "Widespread 'Competence Greenwashing' Threatens to Derail Progress in Sustainable Finance," *The Hill*, June 25, 2021, https://thehill.com/changing-america/sustainability/environment/560255-widespread-competence-greenwashing-threatens-to.

Avery Ellfeldt, "As Investors Try to Be More Ethical, Some Find No Escape from Businesses They Detest," NPR, October 26, 2019, https://www.npr.org/2019/10/26/771323268/as-investors-try-to-be-more-ethical-some-find-no-escape-from-businesses-they-det.

Dominic Rushe, "Green Investing 'Is Definitely Not Going to Work', Says Ex-BlackRock Executive," *The Guardian*, March 30, 2021, https://www.theguardian.com/business/2021/mar/30/tariq-fancy-environmentally-friendly-green-investing.

Rebecca Steel, "Three Steps Toward Sustainability That Every Business Should Be Taking," *Forbes*, July 26, 2021, https://www.forbes.com/sites/forbesbusinesscouncil/2021/07/26/three-steps-toward-sustainability-that-every-business-should-be-taking/?sh=4ac9a2bf3068.

Paul Sullivan, "Investing in Social Good Is Finally Becoming Profitable," *New York Times*, August 28, 2020, https://www.nytimes.com/2020/08/28/your-money/impact-investing-coronavirus.html.

For Further Discussion

Chapter 1
1. What are some of the main challenges associated with transitioning the workforce for a green economy? Are some of these challenges more difficult than others to manage?
2. What steps can governments take to help workers prepare for the greener economies of the future?
3. What steps can parents and educators take and what kinds of information can they provide to children and young adults to help them prepare for a greener job market as they enter the workforce?

Chapter 2
1. What do advocates of green reform plans like the GND mean when they argue that such efforts will pay for themselves over time?
2. What are some of the industries that stand to benefit and grow in the wake of green reform? What industries are likely to experience decline as the world moves toward a cleaner, more sustainable economy?
3. What are the pros and cons of financing green reform with tax increases? How do they compare to the pros and cons of financing green reform with deficit spending?

Chapter 3

1. What are the core ideas associated with the degrowth movement and how do they relate to the broader issues associated with green reform?
2. How does the ongoing political controversy over green reform impact the United States' power and position on the international stage?
3. How does the current growth rate of green industries compare to the growth rate of fossil fuel industries?

Chapter 4

1. What are some of the characteristics that green-minded consumers and investors should look for when deciding whether to do business with a company?
2. What are some of the business opportunities available to entrepreneurs who want to participate in the movement toward a green economy?
3. What are some of the challenges that small businesses may face during the transition to a green economy?

Organizations to Contact

The editors have compiled the following list of organizations concerned with the issues debated in this book. The descriptions are derived from materials provided by the organizations. All have publications or information available for interested readers. The list was compiled on the date of publication of the present volume; the information provided here may change. Be aware that many organizations take several weeks or longer to respond to inquiries, so allow as much time as possible.

Berkeley Roundtable on International Economy

330 Sutardja Dai Hall
Berkeley, CA 94720
website: http://brie.berkeley.edu/BRIE

BRIE is an interdisciplinary research project that focuses on the interactions of international economic competition and the development and application of advanced technologies. BRIE's research concentrates on the different ways industrialized economies create competitive advantage and how these differences affect international economic and political relations.

Brighter Green

165 Court Street, #171
Brooklyn, NY 11201
(212) 414-2339, ext. 15
website: www.brightergreen.org

Brighter Green is a public policy action tank that works to raise awareness of and encourage policy action on issues that span the environment, animals, and sustainability. Brighter Green works in the US and internationally with a focus on the countries of the global south and a strong commitment to ensuring and expanding equity and rights.

Environmental Defense Fund

1875 Connecticut Avenue NW, Suite 600
Washington, DC 20009
(800) 684-3322
website: www.edf.org

The Environmental Defense Fund is a nonprofit environmental advocacy group known for its work on issues including global warming, ecosystem restoration, oceans, and human health, and advocates using sound science, economics, and law to find environmental solutions that work.

Global Green

520 Broadway, Suite 200
Santa Monica, CA 90401
(310) 581-2700
email: sustainability@globalgreen.org
website: www.globalgreen.org

Global Green is a think tank working to address some of the greatest challenges facing humanity. Its work is primarily focused on fighting global climate change through its green affordable housing initiatives, National Green Schools Initiative, national and regional green building policies, advocacy, and education.

Intergovernmental Panel on Climate Change

c/o World Meteorological Organization
7 bis Avenue de la Paix
C.P. 2300
CH - 1211 Geneva 2, Switzerland
email: IPCC-Sec@wmo.int
website: www.ipcc.ch

The Intergovernmental Panel on Climate Change (IPCC) is the international body for assessing the science related to climate change. The IPCC was set up in 1988 by the World Meteorological Organization (WMO) and the United Nations Environment

Programme (UNEP) to provide policymakers with regular assessments of the scientific basis of climate change, its impacts and future risks, and options for adaptation and mitigation.

National Academy of Sciences

500 Fifth Street NW
Washington, DC 20001
(202) 334-2000
website: www.nasonline.org

The National Academy of Sciences (NAS) is a private, nonprofit society of distinguished scholars. Established by an act of Congress, signed by President Abraham Lincoln in 1863, the NAS is charged with providing independent, objective advice to the nation on matters related to science and technology.

The Science Coalition

PO Box 65694
Washington, DC 20036
email: sciencecoalition@hudsonlake.com
website: www.sciencecoalition.org

The Science Coalition is a nonprofit, nonpartisan organization of more than 50 leading public and private research universities. It is dedicated to sustaining the federal government's investment in basic scientific research as a means to stimulate the economy, spur innovation, and drive America's global competitiveness.

Union of Concerned Scientists

Two Brattle Square
Cambridge, MA 02138
(617) 547-5552
website: www.ucsusa.org

The Union of Concerned Scientists puts rigorous, independent science to work to solve our planet's most pressing problems. Joining with people across the country, it combines technical analysis and effective advocacy to create innovative, practical solutions for a healthy, safe, and sustainable future.

United States Environmental Protection Agency

1200 Pennsylvania Avenue NW
Washington, DC 20460

(202) 564-4700
website: www.epa.gov

The United States Environmental Protection Agency (EPA) is an agency of the federal government that was created for the purpose of protecting human health and the environment by writing and enforcing regulations based on laws passed by Congress.

Weidenbaum Center on the Economy, Government, and Public Policy

Washington University
MSC 1027-228-170
One Brookings Drive
St. Louis, MO 63130-4899
website: http://wc.wustl.edu

The Weidenbaum Center supports scholarly research, public affairs programs, and other activities in the fields of economics, government, and public policy.

Bibliography of Books

Max Ajl. *A People's Green New Deal.* London, UK: Pluto Press, 2021.

Sandra L. Albro. *Vacant to Vibrant: Creating Successful Green Infrastructure Networks.* Washington, DC: Island Books, 2019.

Noam Chomsky and Robert Pollin. *Climate Crisis and the Global Green New Deal.* New York, NY: Verso, 2020.

Danny Cullenward and David G. Victor. *Making Climate Policy Work.* Medford, MA: Polity Press, 2020.

Daniel J. Fiorino. *A Good Life on a Finite Earth: The Political Economy of Green Growth.* New York, NY: Oxford University Press, 2018.

Bill Gates. *How to Avoid a Climate Disaster: The Solutions We Have and the Breakthroughs We Need.* New York, NY: Knopf, 2021.

Al Gore. *An Inconvenient Truth.* New York, NY: Rodale Books, 2006.

Mathew Hampshire-Waugh. *Climate Change and the Road to Net-Zero.* London, UK: Crowstone Publishing, 2021.

Robert C. Hockett. *Financing the Green New Deal: A Plan of Action and Renewal.* Cham, Switzerland: Palgrave Macmillan / Springer Nature Switzerland AG, 2020.

Andrew J. Hoffman. *How Culture Shapes the Climate Change Debate.* Stanford, CA: Stanford University Press, 2015.

Van Jones. *The Green Collar Economy: How One Solution Can Fix Our Two Biggest Problems.* New York, NY: HarperCollins, 2008.

Naomi Klein. *This Changes Everything: Capitalism vs. The Climate.* New York, NY: Simon & Schuster, 2014.

Bibliography of Books

Thomas M. Kostigen. *Hacking Planet Earth: How Geoengineering Can Help Us Reimagine the Future.* New York, NY: Tarcherperigree, 2020.

Lisa Ann Mandle, Zhiyun Ouyang, James Edwin Salzman, and Gretchen Cara Daily, eds. *Green Growth That Works: Natural Capital Policy and Finance Mechanisms Around the World.* Washington, DC: Island Press, 2019.

Matto Mildenberger. *Carbon Captured: How Business and Labor Control Climate Politics.* Cambridge, MA: MIT Press, 2020.

Adrian Newton and Elena Cantarello. *An Introduction to the Green Economy: Science, Systems, and Sustainability.* New York, NY: Routledge, 2014.

William D. Nordhaus. *The Climate Casino: Risk, Uncertainty, and Economics for a Warming World.* New Haven, CT: Yale University Press, 2013.

Bill Nye. *Unstoppable: Harnessing Science to Change the World.* New York, NY: St. Martin's Griffin, 2015.

Varshini Prakash and Guido Girgenti, eds. *Winning the Green New Deal: Why We Must, How We Can.* New York, NY: Simon and Schuster, 2020.

Jeremy Rifkin. *The Green New Deal: Why the Fossil Fuel Civilization Will Collapse by 2028 and the Bold Economic Plan to Save Life on Earth.* New York, NY: St. Martin's Griffin, 2019.

Per Espen Stoknes. *Tomorrow's Economy: A Guide to Creating Healthy Green Growth.* Cambridge, MA: MIT Press, 2021.

Maya K. Van Rossum. *The Green Amendment: Securing Our Right to a Healthy Environment.* New York, NY: Disruption Books, 2017.

Index

A

Ameduri, Kenneth, 123

B

Bacardi, 154
Barbier, Edward, 43, 45–49
Benveniste, Alexis, 147
Biden, Joe/Biden administration, 14, 18, 25–27, 43, 51, 52, 53, 124, 125, 126, 127, 131, 137
Biggs, Chris, 111, 138–143
Build Back Better initiative, 14, 18, 25–27, 43, 124

C

cap-and-trade system, 50, 51, 52, 59, 121
carbon pricing, 50–61
carbon tax, 48–49, 50, 51, 52, 57, 58, 60, 66, 76, 121, 140
CARES Act, 129, 130
Carley, Sanya, 159–164
Carter, Sophie, 105–108
China, 22, 34, 53, 60, 66, 93, 97, 99, 100, 116, 123
Coca-Cola, 152
COVID-19 pandemic, 53, 85, 86, 107, 111, 124, 125, 127, 129, 130, 131, 136, 137, 139, 140, 142, 143

D

Dale, Gareth, 94–104
degrowth movement/policies, 79, 81–89
DiPasquale, Christina, 20–24, 79

E

Economic Injury Disaster Loans, 129
Eileen Fisher, 158
Elderson, Frank, 115
energy service companies (ESCOs), 111, 159, 162–163

F

Fischer, Carolyn, 50–61
fossil fuel industry, 90, 92–93, 97, 107

G

Georgeson, Lucien, 90–93
Gordon, Kate, 20–24, 79
green economy
  and challenges for small businesses, 124–137
  and economic growth, 90–93, 94–101
  fundamental skills needed for, 28–32
  investment in, 111–112, 113–117, 118–123, 138–143

Index

and job creation/job loss, 18–19, 20–24, 25–27, 37–40, 90–93, 107, 161

Greenfield, Deborah, 23

green goods, high price of, 147

Green New Deal
  expected costs of, 34, 46–47, 62, 64
  provisions/basics of, 52, 63–64, 74, 97, 114, 120–121

H

Habib, Rishad, 144–158
Hardisty, David J., 144–158
Hayward, Steven F., 72–76
Hazlitt, Henry, 27

I

IKEA, 153
intention-action gap, 145
Ivanova, Irina, 147

J

Jack Daniel's, 148
Jacobsen, Grant, 50–61
Jobs and Neighborhood Investment Act, 130

K

Kahn, Michael, 118–123
Kochhar, Rakesh, 28–32
Konisky, David, 159–164
Kristof, John, 62–66
Kuralbayeva, Karlygash, 37–40

L

Lashitew, Addisu, 124–137
Lonely Whale, 154
Loris, Nicolas, 33–36

M

Mainstreet Lending Program, 125, 130, 131, 133
Markey, Ed, 45, 46, 49, 51, 54, 97, 105, 106, 114, 119
Maslin, Mark, 90–93
Mathai, Manu V., 94–104
Mazzucato, Mariana, 115
Modern Monetary Theory, 65
Mondelez, 141

N

Nestlé, 141
New Deal (1930s), 68, 69, 72, 73, 76, 119

O

Ocasio-Cortez, Alexandria, 45, 46, 49, 51, 62, 63, 64–65, 66, 68, 72, 73, 74, 93, 97, 105, 106, 114, 119, 160

P

P&G, 141, 143
Patagonia, 158
Paterson, Matthew, 14, 67–71
Paycheck Protection Program (PPP), 125, 129, 130–131
Pollin, Robert, 81–89

Polumbo, Brad, 25–27
Polychroniou, C. J., 81–89
Puppim de Oliveira, Jose A., 94–104

R

Reclaiming Appalachia Coalition, 162

S

Sanders, Bernie, 34, 52
Singh, Nidhi, 111, 138–143
Small Business Administration, 125, 128, 129, 130, 132, 133, 136
  Grants, 129
  Loan Forgiveness Program, 130
Small Business Green Recovery Fund, 124–137
Small Business Lending Program, 129
Smith, Adam, 96
South Korea, 47, 100, 139–140
State Small Business Credit Initiative, 129
Stern, Nicholas, 55
Stewart, Daniel, 113–117
Stiglitz, Joseph, 54–55
subscription-based energy programs, 111, 159, 162

T

Trump, Donald/Trump administration, 68, 76, 90, 91, 92–93

U

Unilever, 155
Unnikrishnan, Shalini, 111, 138–143

V

Vincent, Austin, 123

W

Whipple, Alex, 97
White, Katherine, 144–158
World Wildlife Fund, 150